Small Boat Building

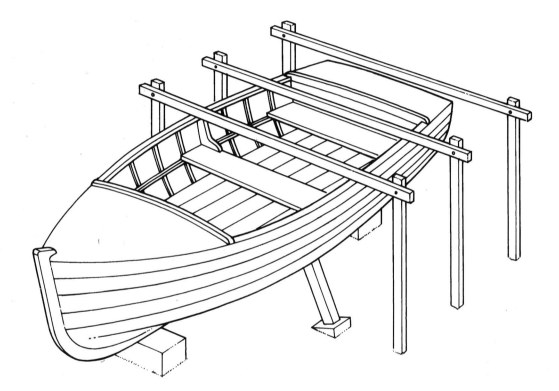

SMALL
BOAT BUILDING

DAVID K. GREENWELL

The Crowood Press

First published in 1997 by
The Crowood Press Ltd
Ramsbury, Marlborough
Wiltshire SN8 2HR

British Library Cataloguing-in-Publication Data
A catalogue record for this book is available from the British Library.

ISBN 1 85223 931 X

Acknowledgements
I would like to acknowledge all the designers, builders and authors,
especially Howard I. Chapelle, Geoffrey Prout, Percy Blandford and Iain
Oughtred for providing inspiration, and also Timber Research and
Development Association for their advice on the proper use of timber.

Dedication
I dedicate this book to my wife, Linda, without whose patience with my
obsession with small boats, and gentle encouragement, the work would
never have taken shape.

Typeface used: Palatino.

Typeset and designed by
D & N Publishing
Membury Business Park, Lambourn Woodlands
Hungerford, Berkshire.

Printed and bound by WBC Book Manufacturers Ltd, Mid Glamorgan.

Contents

Introduction

The purpose of this book is to encourage all those who have dreamt of building their own small boat, to go and prepare their tools and set to work. I believe that provided he or she is not over-ambitious, anyone prepared to devote time to discovering how boats are constructed and to developing a basic knowledge of woodworking, can build a perfectly sound boat. And with a little extra care and understanding, that boat can become not only a joy to build, but a constant source of satisfaction.

This indefinable something that distinguishes an ordinary boat from one with grace and beauty has nothing to do with the professional status or otherwise of the builder; it is more to do with care, enthusiasm and a genuine love of boat building. Many really beautiful boats have been built by amateur builders to a standard that far exceeds anything they could have afforded had it been built by a professional. I am deliberately not making any distinction between those who build boats for money and those who do so for pure enjoyment, because there is no difference. I have never yet met a committed boatbuilder, whatever his status, who is not totally in love with what he is doing. And once the boat is built, she continues to give that feeling of pride and fulfilment in having created something that seems almost alive.

Once you have decided to commit yourself to constructing your own boat, one of the first questions to resolve is, what she should be built from. Not so long ago, the answer would almost certainly have been glass-reinforced plastic, or GRP as it is more commonly known. For the amateur builder, this would probably have meant buying a manufactured hull and fitting it out with timber. Whilst there is undeniable satisfaction in taking that path, many have now come to regard GRP as a rather dead material, somewhat lacking in warmth. The reaction has been a rediscovery of wood, and many now believe that wood is the only option that will provide the satisfaction they are seeking in boat building.

However, this has not just been a nostalgic search to re-establish old values. Due mainly to advances in glues and resins, especially epoxy resin, timber boat construction has undergone a revolution that must surely equal, if not surpass, the developments that, some forty years ago, signalled the decline of wood as the most common boat-building material.

What's wrong with plastic boats? Of course, the answer is nothing, apart that is, from the feeling that it does not provide the 'warmth' timber can give. You see this reaction at boat shows. Watch the passing crowds carefully: individuals will approach a plastic boat and one of the first things they do is to tap on its side with their knuckles. Then the same people will stroke the planking of a wooden boat. Wood is a very tactile material which man has used for thousands of years for shelter, warmth and cooking, and for building boats. We know instinctively that wood is good.

But apart from the pure joy of making something in wood, does it have any real advantages over GRP, which at one time was thought to be virtually indestructible? For a start, wood is lighter. It was Uffa Fox who said words to the effect that weight is only desirable if you are building a steamroller, and this is particularly so for small boats. Then there is the cost. If you are a manufacturer planning to build hundreds of identical boats, then GRP begins to make economic sense – but investing in expensive moulds to build one boat does not. If you really want a GRP-hulled boat, however, the sensible option is to buy a bare hull and fit her out yourself; that way you leave the unpleasant part of the operation to someone else and you don't drive your neighbours to distraction with the smell of styrene. GRP is in fact far from being indestructible and a whole new industry has evolved simply to rectify the problems that can beset this material.

For many, however, the real satisfaction and excitement that stems from building a boat comes from seeing her grow from a pile of timber in the corner of a shed into a craft that is both functional and beautiful.

Finally, one vitally important point – and the reason why I limited this book to the building of small boats – is that one of the biggest traps awaiting the inexperienced boatbuilder is the temptation to be too ambitious. The word to watch out for is 'just': 'Why don't we just make her a couple of feet longer?', or, 'Why don't we just add a small cabin?'. Taken separately, these 'justs' may seem quite innocent – and so they are. But put them together and they soon add up to twice the work, taking three times as long and costing far more than you originally budgeted for. The old adage about not running before you can walk is doubly true when it comes to boat building; and please don't be persuaded that the person who builds the boat that is twice as big, will get double the satisfaction. A well built and carefully finished pram dinghy can bring every bit as much satisfaction as building a fifteen- or twenty-footer (4.5 or 6m). And the feeling of satisfaction and pride does not end with the last coat of varnish: it continues and indeed increases every time you take her afloat.

1 Design

There was a time when small boats were not designed as in the true sense of the word: they simply evolved, the builder basing his latest craft on the one that went before, on local tradition, and on the way his father built before him. Now, there are very few who can draw on generations of handed-down skill and inherited wisdom. So where do we start?

In many ways we have a great advantage over the traditional boatbuilder of the past. We are not bound by any such customs, therefore need not be limited by any one particular type of boat. We are free to draw inspiration from these old-time builders by reading books describing a great variety of small, traditional working boats, by visiting museums, and by keeping our eyes open when travelling through areas where traditional boatyards still exist. This way, the would-be boat builder can develop an eye for a pretty hull shape.

We begin with a dream … an idea … a picture in the imagination, of a little craft dancing on the water. Once we have identified our perfect boat, we can then begin the rewarding and exciting journey towards transforming our dream into reality. For those without any previous boat-building experience, this will be the long yet enjoyable task which must begin by developing an eye for simple, unsophisticated craft. And cast your net wide. As well as British craft, look at those from other lands. The Netherlands and America have strong traditions of simple, small open boats.

TRANSFORMING THE DREAM TO REALITY

There are three options: we can search boatyards, creeks and estuaries for a boat similar to the one we intend building, set to work with a sketchpad and camera, and make a copy. Provided you do this with the owner's permission, and you don't intend going into production, nobody should mind too much.

Another approach is to seek out boat designers – they advertise in many of the yachting magazines – and buy a stock design. There are a number of designers who specialize in offering plans for both professional and amateur builders, and who offer full and straightforward explanations of how to build the boat.

The third option is perhaps the most exciting and rewarding, although it is a path which you tread with great care: that is to design the boat yourself. There are excellent books on this subject, one of which is part of this series, so I don't intend to delve deeply into all aspects of boat design. However, an examination of boat building would not be complete without some reference to the various approaches to design that have been used over the generations, together with a look at the influence modern techniques and technology have had on the subject.

Even the most simple boat has a surprisingly complex and subtle three-dimensional shape, which must be fully understood before building can take place.

Contemporary naval architects (boat designers) use line drawings and tables of offsets to represent hull shape, but this has not always been the case. Before boat design became a separate discipline from boat building, the boatbuilder would make a half-model: a carved wooden representation of one side of the hull made to a convenient scale.

CONSTRUCTING A HALF-MODEL

The half-model served a dual role: it showed a prospective owner just what the boat or ship that he was ordering would look like; and it enabled the builder to develop the lines of the hull. He could then measure off the shape of the moulds and frames over which the hull would be planked.

Due to the high level of competition between builders, many of these half-models became very elaborate and have since become highly prized collectors' items. However, it is not the collectable aspect we are concerned with, but the purely practical way – even in our high-tech world – that a half-model can still be a useful tool, especially to those who are still developing their skills of visualizing the shape and line of a hull. And even though the majority of half-models we see displayed in museums are those of ships, the information gained from building a half-model of even the simplest flat-bottomed dinghy or dory can be a great help when it comes to developing the shape on paper. Certainly for anyone planning on building to their own design, making a half-model is an excellent starting-point.

At first sight, many half-models simply look like half a hull carved from a solid block of wood. But whilst some were that basic, others contain far more information, simply because they were constructed of horizontal layers built up in the form of a multi-layered sandwich. The thickness of

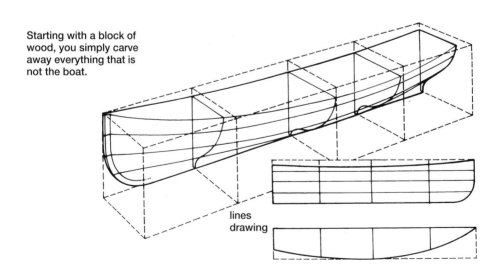

Starting with a block of wood, you simply carve away everything that is not the boat.

lines drawing

Half-model.

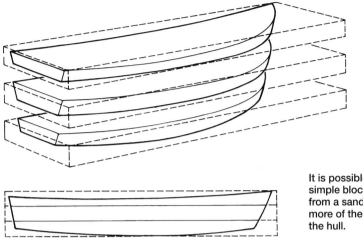

It is possible to start with a simple block but working from a sandwich reveals far more of the character of the hull.

Sandwich construction of simple flat-bottomed dinghy half-model.

each layer – is not just random: they are not made from any convenient old scrap timber lying about the workshop. In fact, each lift should represent the depth between waterlines.

What are these waterlines? Very simply, there are two types: the load waterline, which is the line where the water is expected to reach when the boat is afloat, and the secondary waterlines which are equally spaced above and below, and run parallel to the load-waterline. When it comes to drawing the hull on paper, they, together with the vertical stations (which we will come to later) serve as references, forming a grid onto which the shape of the hull can be drawn.

Whilst time-served boatbuilders were perhaps able to develop the shape of a half-model from their mind's eye, it is unlikely that a less experienced person could do so without running into problems. So, like most twentieth-century craftsmen, we are perhaps better off starting with a rudimentary sketch of what we would eventually like to build full size.

What Sort of Boat?

Although it may not be your ideal dream boat, we will start with a simple flat-bottomed stem dinghy of about 8ft (2.4m) long and 3ft 9in (1.1m) beam measured at the top of the gunwale. As this is our first project we will assume that she will be built in plywood. We need not, at this stage, decide on the detailed method of construction. The significance of choosing the type of building material is linked with the 8 × 4ft standard size of the plywood sheets.

One last point to decide before putting pencil to paper (or wood) is the scale to which the model will be made. Too small, and it will hide the detail that we are looking for; too large, and even the simplest of hull forms will take forever to carve! My own choice is 1½in (3.7cm) to 1ft (30cm): this will make the model of an 8ft (2.4m) dinghy, just 1ft (30cm) long. But there is an even more important benefit gained from using this scale: it means that ⅛in (3mm) on the model is equivalent to 1in (2.5cm) full size. I make no apology at this stage for using imperial measurements instead of the more modern metric when constructing this type of model. Apart from any other considerations, plywood is still largely sold in 8 × 4ft sheets. Nevertheless, I have nothing against those who wish to work in metric units.

Making a Preliminary Sketch

Ideally, to begin with we would draw two vertical lines on a clean piece of paper, 12in (30cm) apart to represent the overall length of the dinghy to our ⅛in (3mm) scale. Many people find it much easier to make preliminary sketches without being hampered by working within the constraints of a particular scale. Some find it easier to begin by making a free-hand sketch of the dinghy. Start with a sketch, looking from the side; although there are no fixed rules about it, convention dictates that you draw your boat with the bows to the right. When you are satisfied with the overall shape and general proportions, draw in a scale using a set square, straight-edge and a pair of dividers or compasses. Start by drawing in the two vertical lines, one at the stem, the other at the stern, and at 90° to the estimated load-waterline. Then draw a horizontal line between the two verticals, a little way above the hull sketch: this is the base line. From the point where the horizontal line crosses the left-hand vertical line, draw another straight line at about 30° to the horizontal. Using either dividers or compasses, divide the angled line into eight equal steps. The exact distance between these divisions does not matter provided they are equal.

Establishing Scale

In the next step, the important thing is to ensure that your straight-edge is held firmly in place throughout the operation. Place the set square on the paper so that its perpendicular edge passes through the eighth division mark on the angled line, and the point at which the horizontal line passes through the right-hand vertical line (at the bow). Place the straight-edge along the base of the set square, holding it firmly against the paper, and gently slide the set square along until the perpendicular edge that passed through the eighth division, now passes through the seventh. With a sharp pencil, strike a line through the base line.

Still holding the straight-edge firmly in place, slide the set square to station six in the scale line and make another pencil mark through the base line. Repeat the process until each point on the scale line has a corresponding line on the base line. You will now have divided the base line into eight, each division representing 1ft (30cm). You can then further divide the first 1ft(30cm) into four simply by halving it and halving it again, by eye.

Establishing the Basic Design

Using the created scale, it is possible to put dimensions to other parts of your sketch to see how well proportioned it is. Even at this early stage, you may wish to make changes, perhaps in the depth on the hull, the height of the stem and so on. You can also now sketch in a plan view: the shape looking down from above. First draw in a centre line parallel to the base line, and below the side elevation. Decide how broad you want the transom, and draw it in along the left-hand perpendicular, centred about the centre line. We will discuss transom width more fully later; for the moment, it is sufficient to say that what looks right will probably

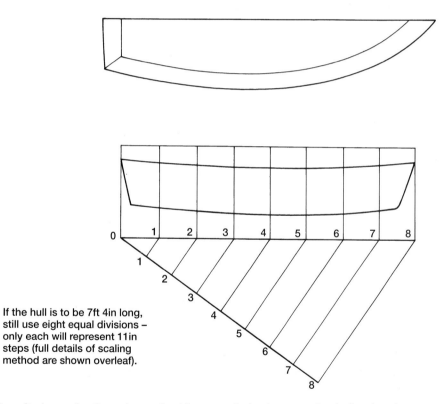

Drawing to a scale of 1:8 = ⅛in to the foot.

If the hull is to be 7ft 4in long, still use eight equal divisions – only each will represent 11in steps (full details of scaling method are shown overleaf).

A preliminary sketch can be made either to scale (top) or completely free-hand as above and scaled off once the proportions have been established.

be right, so we will make it 2ft 9in (84cm) wide at the top.

Having decided on the maximum beam (3ft 9in; 1.1m), consider where it will occur. So the next line to put in the drawing board is a guideline drawn parallel to and half the beam's width on either side of the centre line. There is no need to draw both sides of the hull on the plan, but at this preliminary stage it has the advantage of providing two chances of drawing in a fair curve representing the gunwale.

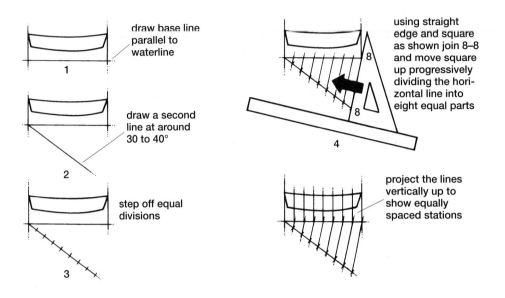

Scaling up a free-hand sketch in preparation to making a half-model or lines drawing to scale.

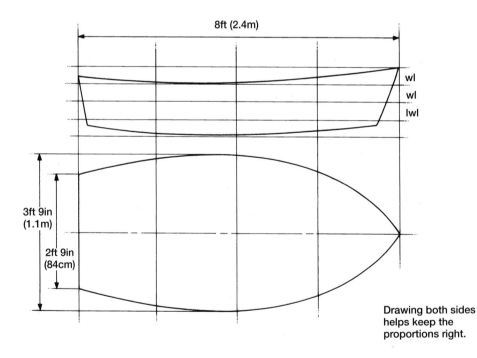

Drawing the proposed half-model to scale against a grid of waterlines.

Drawing the Curve

Now comes the tricky task of drawing the curve. The three main options are: draw it free-hand; draw round a flexible batten; or use a French curve. There are advantages in starting with a free-hand curve, as long as you have the ability to draw a fair curve. It avoids being influenced by the shape of the French curve. Once the line is established by eye, it can then be trued up using a flexible batten or French curve. Now all that remains is to draw in the stations – vertical lines equally spaced between the two perpendiculars.

Drawing in the Waterlines

At this stage we can reproduce our drawing to the scale that we intend to use for the half-model. Also, this is when the waterlines can be drawn in. To start with I simply guess where the load-waterline should be, or at least where I hope it will be; this point can be considered later, when analysing the completed half-model. Once the load-waterline is in, we can draw in the secondary waterlines –

although on a flat-bottomed boat these are really only of academic interest. But it is convenient if they coincide with the thickness of the timber to be used in the half-model.

Cutting Out the Half-model

So far we have only created a very basic, part-finished drawing of our 8ft (2.4m) flattie, but it is enough to enable us to start on the half-model. The secret of success here includes sharp tools, careful marking out and patience; also, always work to a pencil line, and never try to remove more than a shaving at a time.

Start by tracing out the half-plan view onto your timber to make the first lift, allowing ⅛in (3mm) all round for trimming later. Cut the shape out using either a coping saw or electric jigsaw. Because at this stage we have not decided how much flare the sides of the boat will have, make three more identical pieces. The species of timber you use is not really important. Any relatively close-grained, easy-to-carve and knot-free wood will do the job, although geltong, the timber favoured by

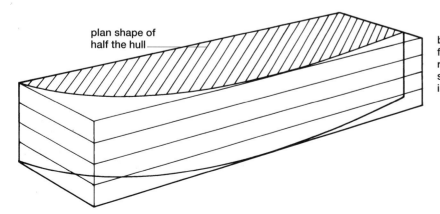

plan shape of half the hull

block made up of four layers, each representing the spacing of the imaginary waterlines

The first cut.

pattern makers, is ideal if you can get it. For economy I have used simple pine, which is not perhaps the best wood for carving, but with care, cuts easily enough.

Mark each station down the back edge of each lift, then glue them together, lining up the station lines on the rear edges to form the blank from which the half-model will be carved. An obvious question at this point is to ask why we went to all the trouble of creating the blank from four layers. Would it not have been easier to have used a 4in (10cm) thick piece of solid timber? No doubt it would, but the resulting model would not give up its secrets half as easily. The glue lines provide a far more accurate grid of parallel lines than could ever be drawn in place after the model has been carved to shape. Furthermore, when making a more sophisticated hull shape, it is possible to screw the lifts together instead of gluing them. This enables the half-model to be taken apart again – an advantage when analysing the model, especially if you intend to make an accurate drawing of the hull's lines.

Once the glue has set hard, the clamps can be removed and the back face of the block trued up to with a lick of a sharp plane, followed by sandpapering on a flat surface. But first, carry the station lines onto the top and bottom faces of the block so that they can be restored after the block has been trued up – and don't forget that only ⅛in (3mm) was allowed for this trimming.

Flare, Sheer and Rocker

Imagine that concealed inside this block of wood is a perfectly formed half-model just waiting to be released: all we have to do is pare away all the surplus wood, and we will be left with the perfect shape. Certainly, in plan our block of wood is starting to look like a boat, but it still lacks three features:

flare, sheer and rocker. Flare is the outward angle of the sides towards the gunwale. sheer is the curve of the gunwale when viewed from the side. To most people's eye, a sheer line that curves up to the bow and stern looks far prettier than a flat of reverse sheer where the gunwale or deck line either remains straight between the tops of transom and bow, or curves down from amidships to the ends of the hull. Rocker is the amount of curve in the keel, or, in the case of a flat-bottomed boat, in the bottom upwards to the transom and bow/stem.

Applying Flare

Returning to our half-model, the first of these three elements to apply is flare. The question is: how much? On a boat of this length I would expect the maximum beam across the bottom to be in the region of 3ft 3in (1m). One could also ask why we need to have flare on a small boat anyway. It is perfectly possible, and far easier to build a boat without, but it does bring certain benefits that many will argue far outweigh the disadvantage of adding complication. First there is the question of simple aesthetics, in that for most people's taste, a small boat with straight up-and-down sides is not very attractive, although there are exceptions. But there are also at least two sound technical reasons for having flare in a boat: it improves the load-carrying capacity, and it makes the boat more stable.

First, mark in pencil the maximum half-beam on the bottom of the block at around the number two station. Then, holding the pencil tightly and using your second and third fingers as a guide, extend the line right round the curve, from stem to stern, and then shade in the section of wood to be cut away. Now, in your mind's eye, imagine what the model will look like with the

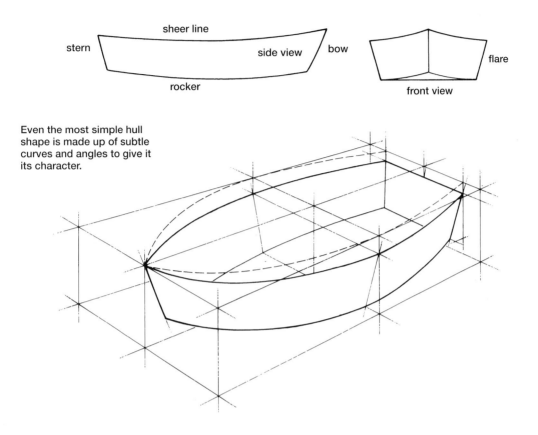

sheer line

stern side view bow flare

rocker

front view

Even the most simple hull shape is made up of subtle curves and angles to give it its character.

Naming the curves and angles.

shaded portion removed. If you are not satisfied with the result, adjust the position of the line accordingly.

Next, pare away at the block until a nice smooth curve is achieved, representing the side of the boat. This operation is made easier if you screw a couple of temporary blocks into the rear and top faces of the model so that it can be held securely in vice with a clear run for chisel and spokeshave. Work progressively from the middle towards the ends, and try to establish the eventual angle right from the start. If you simply hack away at the block in the hope that it will come true in the end, not only do you make it more difficult to create a

constant curve, but you also destroy the satisfaction of seeing the shape develop as you work. Once the pencil line has been reached, it is worth spending time with sandpaper and block to achieve a really smooth curve.

Although there are still two curves to be carved, we can already check whether or not the curve that has been created on the half-model can, in fact, be built from flat sheets of plywood. The rule is that a flat sheet can only be bent in one direction at a time, and although there are exceptions that we will go into later – a technique known as tortured ply construction – at the moment, we will remain loyal to the general principle.

It is possible to make an accurate drawing of the half model and to prove on the drawing-board whether it is, or is not possible to bend the plywood in the way we want: this procedure is called conical projection, and it should be covered in any good book on design. However, there is a much easier way, now that we have our partly completed model: simply take a piece of thin card, the same width as the side of the model, and bend it round; the card should sit snugly without creating any gaps. If there is a gap, don't worry at this stage because it can be dealt with later: in fact it is much more important at this point to create an attractive sheer line.

Establishing the Sheer Line

There are three main reasons for having a curved sheer: two affect the performance of the boat, the other simply influences the way she looks. Imagine your boat being driven into waves, and you will appreciate the importance of having sufficient buoyancy in the bows. That means volume to enable the boat to lift to the wave, and also for the bow to be high enough to prevent the water coming over the top and flooding the boat. Aboard a stem dinghy, the bows are by definition narrow, which means the only way to achieve sufficient volume is to have them relatively high. There is, of course, a further factor which helps the bow lift, and that is the flare: not only does it produce a dynamic lift, it also increases the rate of increase in buoyancy as the bow dips deeper into the water.

If we were to make the middle of the boat the same height above the waterline as the bow, a quick glance at the part-complete half-model clearly shows the result: the volume amidships would be far greater than needs be, and apart from perhaps not

looking very pretty, it would mean extra weight in the topsides which is not good for stability. Also, an excessively large side area would give a high degree of windage, possibly making the boat difficult to control in a side wind.

Regarding the stern of the boat, we are confronted with a similar, although at the same time slightly different situation, from that which exists at the bow. If the boat is travelling through the water with a following sea, the stern should be able to lift in a similar fashion to the bow. The difference is that, unless the craft is canoe-sterned, the stern is usually much wider than the bow; also the weight of a passenger who could be sitting on the stern seat, and perhaps a small outboard engine mounted on the transom must be taken into account. Yet another factor to consider if the boat is to be fitted with an outboard, is the length of the outboard engine's shaft. Finally there is the look of the vessel, in as much as the curve down from the bow to amidships should be balanced by a similar, but not identical, curve upwards towards the transom.

The most economical, and also the easiest sheer line to produce is the one that occurs naturally from the straight-edged panel. This can be drawn directly onto the half-model by first marking the top of the stem and transom and then wrapping a piece of straight-edged stiff card round the side of the model to join the two points with a pencil line.

If the half-model has only a small amount of flare, the resulting sheer may be too flat. Conversely if the flare is generous, as is the case with a dory, then the sheer line may well be over-exaggerated. Either way the solution is simple: draw in a point on the model amidships where you think the gunwale – the top edge of the boat – should come. Measure the difference between the sheer line drawn in using the straight-edged card, and your new mark. Transfer this measurement into the card template, translating it into a curve using a flexible bittern. Cut the curve in the template and then offer it back to the half-model. The new sheer curve may now be drawn in.

It is possible to experiment by changing the template curve to create an asymmetric sheer line. But don't be too adventurous because aboard a small boat, the curves can be relatively tight, creating problems when bending gunwale strakes round on the full-size boat. Here again, the saying 'What looks right' … so keeping it simple.

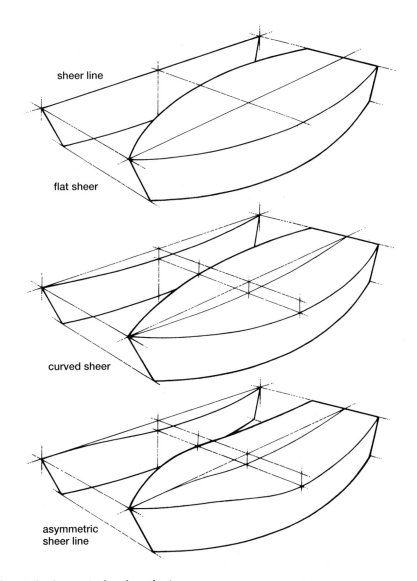

Sheer in a small boat is both practical and aesthetic.

Drawing in the Rocker

Once the sheer line has been drawn in, it is very tempting to forge ahead with cutting it to shape; however, it is far more convenient to draw in the rocker first – the fore-and-aft curve of the bottom of the boat. There are several factors to consider, and we will look at those that are especially relevant to flat-bottomed boats.

When the boat passes through the water, the less disturbance it makes, the easier it will be to propel, and this is important for all boats whether driven by sails, oars or outboard engine. If the hull has a perfectly flat bottom without any rocker, all the

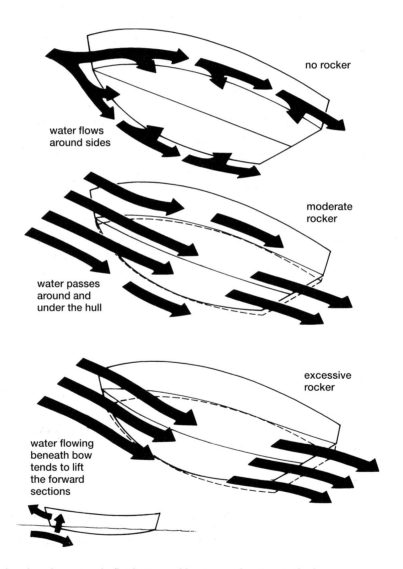

Water flow around and under a simple flat-bottomed boat – moderation is the key.

water that passes by is pushed around either side. If the bottom has a rocker, the water is parted on all three sides so that its parting and closing as the boat passes is smoother. Too much rocker creates an unequal flow round the hull, biased towards the bottom which in the extremes can induce a rocking-horse motion that is not only uncomfortable but also slows the boat down.

There are two further factors we need to consider regarding the effect rocker has on performance before we decide how much curve to put into the bottom of our model. Both involve stability. First, directional stability: obviously we want the boat to travel in a straight line of its own accord and not charge off in any direction, and to this end, a moderate rocker is most effective. But we don't want our boat to hold her course to such an extent that she becomes difficult to turn, especially if she is to carry sails, otherwise it could prove difficult when tacking to windward. Conversely, a boat intended primarily for rowing or for use with an outboard engine has the opposite priority, because

it needs to run in a straight line. The problem begins when you want the boat to both sail and row well. Basically, a balance must be struck, and the solution is to avoid extremes. Perhaps the best way to learn is to emulate examples of past boat building, and often a good source of inspiration in this quest are the examples of inshore working boats which can be seen in many maritime museums around the coast.

The second factor regarding the effect rocker has on performance concerns lateral stability, or the ability to resist capsize; to most boat owners this is the most important characteristic of all. An unballasted, flat-bottomed boat relies almost entirely on its width at the waterline for its lateral stability. The problem is that although this type of boat is initially very stable when floating level, as it heels the waterline beam can be dramatically decreased to the point where the boat is no longer stable and will easily capsize. By providing the right amount of rocker, it is possible to minimize the reduction in waterline beam as the boat heels. However, too much rocker

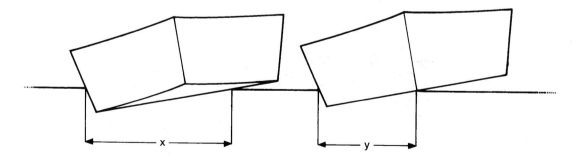

Because the hull with rocker will float deeper in the water when heeled, it will maintain a greater waterline beam (x) than a similar hull but with no rocker (y) and therefore will be more stable.

The effect of rocker on stability as boat heels.

21

has the adverse effect of reducing the waterline length, which can also reduce lateral stability. Again, this serves to underline the desirability of avoiding extremes.

On larger boats – say, 14ft (4.2m) long and above – you can really start to design the shape of the rocker to reduce pounding (the tendency to slam down with a crash in rough water) and to prevent the transom from dragging through the water, one of the most effective ways of slowing any boat. Without going into great detail, the forward third of the bottom should be virtually flat, with the major curve taking place in the last half to one-third of the hull.

Aboard a boat of less than 10ft (3m) in length, however, there is little room for any sophisticated offset rocker, and it is perhaps safest to adopt a gentle, even profile so that when the boat is at rest, both the bottom of the stem and the transom sit just clear of the water. For our model we will assume that to mean an overall rise at both stem and stern of between 3 and 4in (7.6 and 10cm).

Cutting Out the True Shape

Once you are satisfied with the result, the next task is to cut away the waste timber to reveal the true shape. The most effective tool for this job is undoubtedly a fine-toothed bandsaw, but for those who don't possess one, use a tenon saw, a shallow gouge (if you have one), a paring chisel and a sandpaper block complete with copious supplies of sandpaper.

Carefully transfer the sheer and rocker curve to the rear face of the model, remembering that you are transferring perpendicular heights – which simply means, don't confuse the distances down the sides of the model with those down the vertical back face.

To cut the sheer line, either use your bandsaw, or make a series of vertical cuts with the tenon saw along the curves at about 1in (2.5cm) intervals. Using the gouge (or the chisel), pare the waste wood away working from the ends towards the centre, always keeping a keen eye on the lay of the grain. Having cut the curve as accurately as you can, finish off by sanding. Make a sanding block by planing a mating curve into a piece of scrap wood: five minutes sanding by hand should result in a beautifully smooth result.

The rocker can be cut in a similar fashion, but in this case working from the middle of the bottom outwards; this avoids the possibility of the wood splitting along the grain into the model. The next check is to find out if you can get both sides from a single sheet of plywood. Looking back at the half-model, however, there seems to be one point we have forgotten: the angle of the transom. In fact we have not really forgotten it, just left it until later, for reasons that will become clear.

Obviously if the boat were only 7ft 3in (2.2m) in overall length, there would be no problem, but can an 8ft (2.4m) long panel of ply be cut in such a way as to 'stretch' it to take account of the curve. The answer is a guarded 'yes', and the easiest way to find out is to check using the model. The answer lies in the angle, or rake of the stem and stern, which is why we have left the question of transom rake until now.

TRANSOM RAKE

For the sake of simplicity we gave the sides a nearly constant flare angle, and the stem adopted its own angle from the perpendicular quite naturally, it being the function of the two sides coming together. Transom rake, however, is not governed by the fare, and with a little ingenuity the transom angle can be used to provide extra boat length. But maximizing building materials should not take precedence, and at this point it is worth taking a general look at the effect transom angle has on seaworthiness.

Small boat design has been dominated to such a degree by the requirements of outboard engines that one could be forgiven for thinking that the only factor governing the angle of a transom is whether or not such an engine can be clamped in place. However, rowing enthusiasts would argue that a small, well designed dinghy is far more convenient if powered by oar – after all, oars are considerably more environmentally friendly and infinitely cheaper to run. And there are other factors influenced by the rake of the transom: to begin with there is the aesthetic aspect, and here again, visual balance is important – although it is far more subtle than just setting the transom at a complementary angle to the stem. On some boats that is the right course to adopt, but on others – the American flat-bottomed skiff being a prime example – a well raked transom is in perfect harmony with a near vertical or even a plumb stem.

Seaworthiness a Priority

If the boat is to be used in anything but the most sheltered waters, then seaworthiness is a most important consideration. When a boat is being driven into a head sea, the most important feature of the transom is that it does not create drag, and as we have already discussed, on a flat-bottomed boat that is more a function of the bottom rocker than the angle of the transom. However,

when the situation is reversed and the boat is travelling with a following sea and perhaps being overtaken by the waves, transom rake can be every bit as important as sufficient rocker.

Picture, for a moment, the results of a wave hitting the stern of a small boat or dinghy with a reverse angle (retroussé) transom: the bottom edge would most probably dig into the wave, scooping it on board with possibly dire results. The same boat with a vertical transom would fare somewhat better, but it would do little or nothing to encourage the wave to pass beneath the boat. A well raked transom, on the other hand, would generate dynamic lift as the wave surged past, and would also provide increased buoyancy to lift the stern of the boat over the wave, helping to prevent the boat becoming swamped.

It can, of course, be overdone. Too much rake, along with too much buoyancy in the stern, can encourage a boat to dig her bow in and broach, which simply means that when caught by a wave from astern, the stern lifts and the boat accelerates, and like a car going into an uncontrolled skid, the back tries to catch up with the front, causing her to turn sideways on to the wave, possibly resulting in a capsize. The answer is to avoid extremes, and to follow the leads provided by designs that have evolved to deal with such sea conditions.

Cutting Out Procedure

With all this in mind, we can now return to our model. Normally, if we were to cut the sides from one continuous sheet, the plywood removed to form the stem and stern angles would simply be wasted. But by making each side in two parts it is possible to cut the sheets in such a way as to avoid

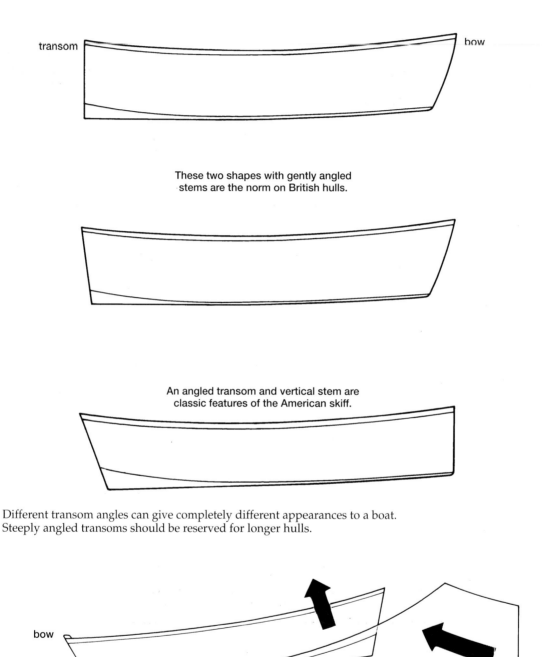

transom   bow

These two shapes with gently angled
stems are the norm on British hulls.

An angled transom and vertical stem are
classic features of the American skiff.

Different transom angles can give completely different appearances to a boat.
Steeply angled transoms should be reserved for longer hulls.

bow

A following sea lifts
an angled transom
more easily.

Wave action from astern.

24

throwing away four triangles of valuable plywood, and at the same time, add at least 1ft (30cm) to the overall length of each side panel. This technique does, however, mean that we have to join the side panels, which involves making either strapped butt or scarf joints. Personally I prefer to use scarf joints, which are not as difficult to make as many would have us believe. The idea is to create the bow angle at the centre of one plywood panel, and the transom angle at the centre of the other. Then marry up the resulting pairs, and join them to form the two handed side panels.

Once the maximum length of side panel has been determined – and this depends very much on the angle of the transom – a template can be cut to scale and bent round the side of the half-model. Its maximum practical length and true transom angle can be drawn in, and the model finished by cutting away the wood beyond the transom.

The half-model can be finished off by further sanding and varnishing, and even by mounting on a handsome back board; however, as a working model it is now complete, and can be measured and scaled to prepare a working drawing. It can even be used as a guide to help make a preliminary plywood-cutting list which will give an indication of initial building cost.

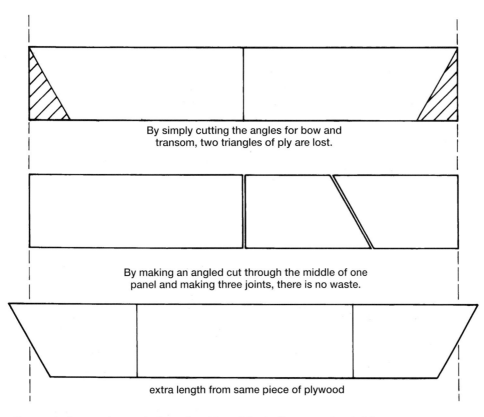

By simply cutting the angles for bow and transom, two triangles of ply are lost.

By making an angled cut through the middle of one panel and making three joints, there is no waste.

extra length from same piece of plywood

Making the most of your plywood – here the sides of the hull are constructed from two 8ft (2.4m) panels.

MORE SOPHISTICATED HALF-MODELS

Although I have given a description of building a half-model of arguably the simplest hull form possible, the same technique can be used to build much more sophisticated hull shapes. In spite of the greater complexity however, a little more preliminary work on the drawing board can make the task of carving the shape far easier, and can also reveal a lot more about the eventual hull shape. Most relevant at this point is the individual shape of each of the lifts that form the sandwich, even on the simple flat-bottomed stem dinghy.

The Preliminary Drawing

Using the same sandwich type of construction as before, start by drawing the waterlines to scale on a sheet of paper, along with a horizontal centre line below on which to draw the plan view, and a vertical centre line to the right of the waterlines for the end view. You can do this using a proper drawing board, but it is probably just as easy, and far more convenient, to make this preliminary drawing on a pad of squared paper.

Drawing the Transom

On the plan view centre line, draw to your chosen scale the overall length, maximum beam and the width of the transom, or the transoms if she is to be a pram dinghy. Project the overall length up to the set of waterlines onto which the side elevation is to be drawn, and sketch in what you think the boat should look like when seen from the side. Now draw in the stations to divide the overall length into, say, four equal parts.

Drawing in the End Views

From the side elevation and plan, it is now possible to begin drawing in the end views, starting with the amidships section which is number two in our plans. Don't worry too much about the sheer line for the moment, as that can be finalized later.

Using a compass, step off the beam at the amidships station, and transfer it to the end-view centre line. Now sketch in the shape you think the section should be. Don't forget that on an unballasted boat, a wide, flat bottom is far more stable than a narrow, rounded one.

Now do the same for station two, projecting across the beam at gunwale level and the depth of the hull, and draw in the shape of the hull in sympathy with station two. Do this on the left-hand side of the centre line which will represent the boat as seen from astern. The view from the bow will be drawn to the right of the centre line, thus avoiding having to draw two end views.

As before, when making the flat-bottomed half-model, the thickness of each lift forming the sandwich will be equal to the depth between each waterline. A glance at the end view on the drawing we have just produced shows clearly the difference in shape between the top and bottom waterlines.

Drawing the Plan View

Now, if we go just one step further with our drawing, we can project the curve of each waterline onto the plan view, which will enable us to make each lift correspond far more closely to its final shape. Take each waterline in turn and step off the beam at each station, including the bow and stern transoms, transferring the dimension to the corresponding station on the plan view. Then carefully join the marks, either by drawing free-hand or using a French curve. Each of these waterline curves should be smooth and in harmony with one another. If one has an unsightly bulge, it is a sign that the shape of one or more of the end view stations is not correct. Resolve the problem by smoothing the curve on the plan view, projecting the result back into the end elevation and adjusting the drawing accordingly.

Cutting Out the Half-model

Once you are satisfied that the curves, or angles in the case of a multi-chine boat, are reasonably fair, attention can be turned towards making a half-model by first cutting out the individual lifts, fastening them together and then carving the resulting blank to shape using broadly the same techniques as employed when making the flat-bottomed half-model.

Put in the sheer line which can either first be sketched in on the drawing, or drawn straight onto the half-model, first on the back face and then projected across the top to the front face.

What You Get from Making a Half-model

Why, some may ask, go to the effort of making a half-model when we have gone to the trouble of drawing the hull first? It is important to remember that we only made a sketch, even though it needed considerable care to produce something from which we could take rough measurements. To develop anything but the most simple hull

forms on paper to the point at which one could be confident that it would translate directly into a full-size boat is probably beyond the abilities of somebody new to boat building: it is a process needing skill and experience. By making a half-model, however, any mistakes in the drawing quickly become apparent and can be corrected before they become costly errors. But more than that, making a half-model provides a valuable opportunity to become familiar with the shape of a hull, with its subtle curves which blend to create a shape that is both beautiful and functional.

Making a half-model to investigate one's own design is only part of the story: it is equally valuable, and can provide just as many answers if you are setting out to build a boat from a set of plans purchased from a professional designer. The only difference is that instead of creating the hull shape from one's own imagination, you must use your skill to reproduce the shape created by the designer and which leaves no room for improvisation. This is done in much the same way as we have already discussed, starting by scaling the distance between the waterlines, and building up the sandwich of lifts cut to the plan shape of the waterlines. This time, however, the blank must be carved accurately using templates traced off the end view on the hull drawing.

WORKING MODELS

It is possible to learn virtually all we need to know about the shape of a boat from building, studying and preparing drawings from a half-model. However, even more information can be gleaned from also building a working scale model before committing oneself to building a

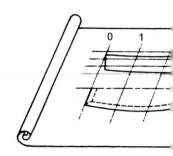

Stage 1 Draw the basic grid of waterlines (the pieces of timber that make up the sandwich) and lines marking the overall length and centre line of end view.

Stage 2 Draw the sheer plan (side profile) the vertical stations and the plan (looking down on the gunwale). Sketch in the chine line in light pencil.

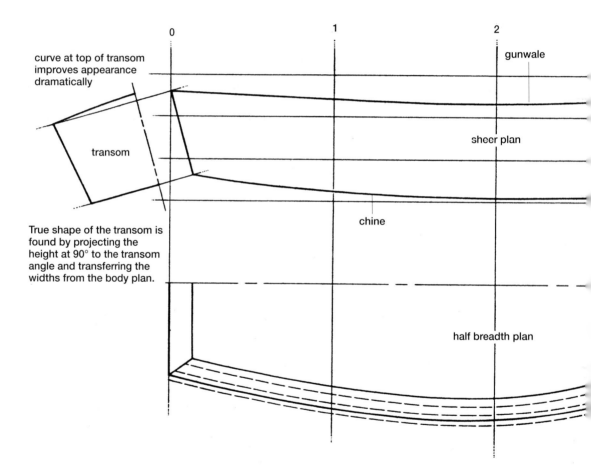

curve at top of transom improves appearance dramatically

transom

True shape of the transom is found by projecting the height at 90° to the transom angle and transferring the widths from the body plan.

gunwale

sheer plan

chine

half breadth plan

Putting a simple hull shape on paper; the next stage is making a model.

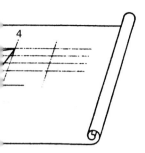

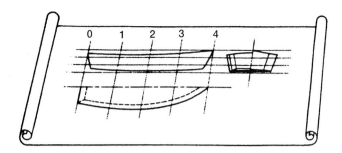

Stage 3 Draw the end view (body plan). This is done by transferring the heights of the stations 0, 1, 2, and 3, and the station beams.

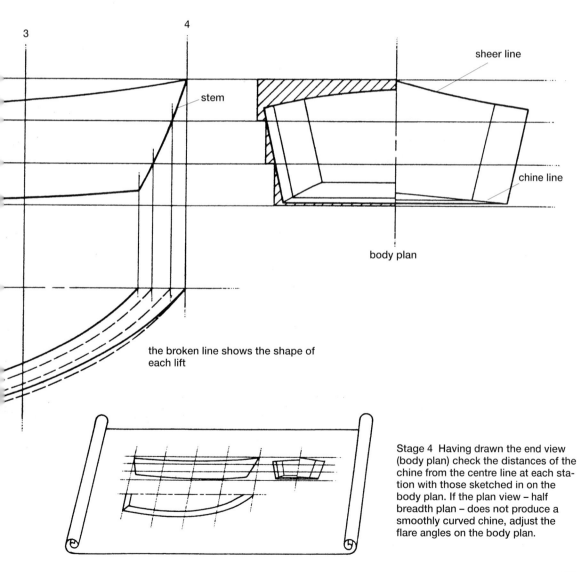

sheer line

stem

chine line

body plan

the broken line shows the shape of each lift

Stage 4 Having drawn the end view (body plan) check the distances of the chine from the centre line at each station with those sketched in on the body plan. If the plan view – half breadth plan – does not produce a smoothly curved chine, adjust the flare angles on the body plan.

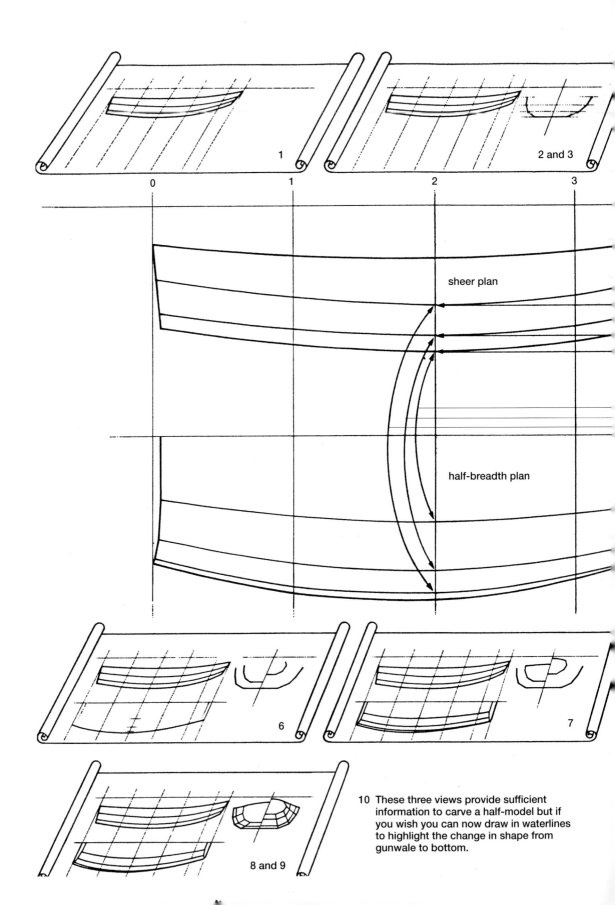

1

2 and 3

0   1   2   3

sheer plan

half-breadth plan

6

7

8 and 9

10 These three views provide sufficient
information to carve a half-model but if
you wish you can now draw in waterlines
to highlight the change in shape from
gunwale to bottom.

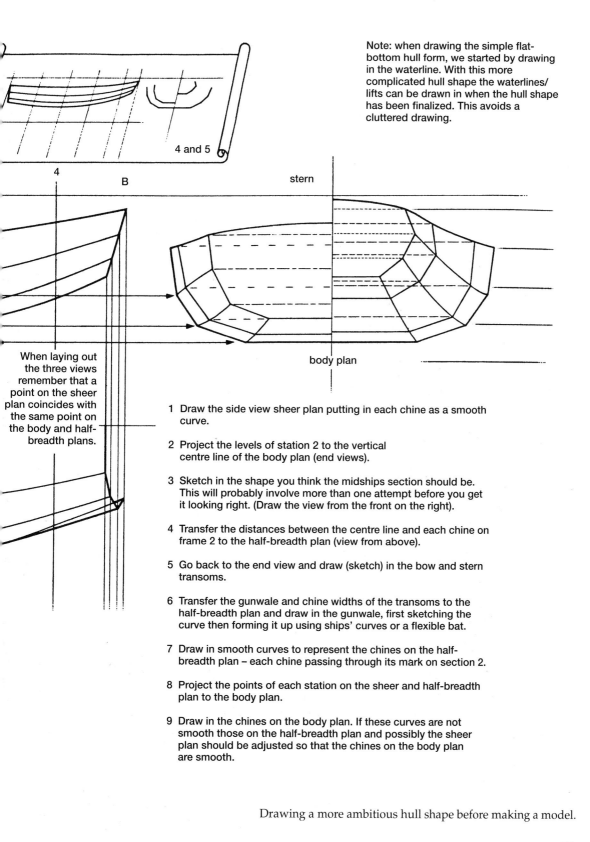

Note: when drawing the simple flat-bottom hull form, we started by drawing in the waterline. With this more complicated hull shape the waterlines/lifts can be drawn in when the hull shape has been finalized. This avoids a cluttered drawing.

4 and 5

4

B

stern

body plan

When laying out the three views remember that a point on the sheer plan coincides with the same point on the body and half-breadth plans.

1 Draw the side view sheer plan putting in each chine as a smooth curve.

2 Project the levels of station 2 to the vertical centre line of the body plan (end views).

3 Sketch in the shape you think the midships section should be. This will probably involve more than one attempt before you get it looking right. (Draw the view from the front on the right).

4 Transfer the distances between the centre line and each chine on frame 2 to the half-breadth plan (view from above).

5 Go back to the end view and draw (sketch) in the bow and stern transoms.

6 Transfer the gunwale and chine widths of the transoms to the half-breadth plan and draw in the gunwale, first sketching the curve then forming it up using ships' curves or a flexible bat.

7 Draw in smooth curves to represent the chines on the half-breadth plan – each chine passing through its mark on section 2.

8 Project the points of each station on the sheer and half-breadth plan to the body plan.

9 Draw in the chines on the body plan. If these curves are not smooth those on the half-breadth plan and possibly the sheer plan should be adjusted so that the chines on the body plan are smooth.

Drawing a more ambitious hull shape before making a model.

full size. And this is again equally true whether proving your own design or learning about a stock design.

Building such a model to the standard that can be seen in many maritime museums is, of course, a highly skilled job; nevertheless the efforts of an amateur can be just as rewarding and valuable in terms of information gained and techniques explored. Provided a workable scale is selected – I favour ⅛in (3mm) to 1ft (30cm), although a larger scale is perhaps better for small dinghies – most of the constructional details can be reproduced in perfect miniature, and those which are just too intricate to reproduce to scale are at least highlighted and can be thought about in advance.

In addition to investigating how each individual component fits and marries with its neighbour, making a scale model allows us to explore the relationship between the shapes of individual planks or panels, and the way those shapes influence the final form of the hull. Some modern construction techniques make this very clear, other more traditional types of hull tend to disguise the effect plank or panel shape has on the eventual outcome.

Back to Basics

Returning to our original example of a flat-bottomed dinghy of about 8ft (2.4) overall length, if you have already made a half-model, it is relatively straightforward to use it to trace off the side, bottom and transom in thin card. The components can then be joined together using adhesive tape to produce a very presentable scale model of the hull shape of the full-size dinghy it is intended to represent. If all goes well, why not go one step further and build your model in thin balsa wood.

The Effect of Flare

In addition to enabling you to see more easily the way the panels fit together, the big advantage a scale model has over its solid, half-model counterpart is that it can be used to investigate the effect altering the flare has on the overall shape of the hull. Add just a little to the beam by giving her more flare amidships, and you will see the dramatic effect it has on the shape and degrees of rocker that is induced into the bottom of the boat. It is also intriguing to see the effect of the curve on the bottom edge of the side panels. Looking at the assembled hull, it would be easy to imagine that it would be a simple, smooth curve. One could also be forgiven for thinking that it would be slightly convex. In reality, however, it is more likely to be a slightly 's'-shaped concave curve.

Understanding Design

Once you have made one model and established the basic shape of the four main components, it is then an easy matter to adjust the curves very slightly with the careful use of scissors in order to explore fully, and begin to understand exactly, what makes a boat the shape she is. The more sophisticated the shape of the hull, the more intricate are the shapes of the panels which go into its building.

The same techniques can be used if the boat is to be built of solid timber planks rather than plywood sheets. And although commercially available boat plans, suitable for the inexperienced boatbuilder, often come with very full details of the dimensions to which the individual panels must be cut, building a scale model is still worthwhile. Not only does it give a far better understanding of the design, it can also save expensive mistakes by perhaps high-lighting the feature of the design that only reveals its true purpose when the hull is finally assembled. It also avoids the temp-tation to correct mistakes that don't exist.

As regards altering a designer's work, my advice is a very positive 'don't': either develop your own ideas from scratch and accept the results as being your own, or accept totally the advice and guidance of the designer whose design you have bought.

At this stage you will no doubt be very keen to make a start on the real thing, but I would suggest that having perfected the shape of your model in card, you now reproduce it in thin plywood, or even balsa wood. The extra stiffness and less forgiving nature of wood will certainly highlight any problems that the flexibility of card may mask. It will also give an opportunity to investigate some of the finer details such as a keel, rubbing strakes, internal framing, thwarts and some form of built-in buoyancy.

Putting Her on Paper

The following section is primarily aimed at those who have decided to build a sim-ple boat to their own design; however, it also aims to unravel some of the more mysterious jargon adopted by naval architects to describe what they do. So even if you are building from a set of bought plans, bear with me whilst I attempt to simplify what some seem to delight in complicating.

Having first carved a half-model and then gone on to make a scale working model of the craft you intend building, it is now well worth the trouble of making working drawings. A naval architect will prepare a whole pile of drawings just for

one boat: for the moment we confine our-selves to two, the lines drawing and the construction plans. The main purpose of the lines drawing is to record, for easy ref-erence, the shape and overall dimension of the boat; to accompany this comes a table of offsets, which we will consider in due course.

The construction plan gives details of the way in which the boat is built and the positioning of the many components that together make the completed craft. It can also give details of materials and 'scant-lings' – the traditional way of referring to the thickness of the timbers used in the boat's construction, but which has now become accepted as referring to the thick-ness/size of the components that go into the building of the hull.

LINES DRAWING

If you are simply making this record for your own use, the way in which you orga-nize the drawing does not really matter. But there are conventions used by profes-sional designers which enable the lines of the boat to be recorded in an ordered fash-ion so that, hopefully, details are not missed, and the information can be easily understood by others. If the newcomer to boat building is to progress to building more complex, professionally designed craft, it is essential that he or she becomes familiar with these conventions. Although they may at first look complicated, they are only a shorthand method of recording the details of a three-dimensional shape on a two-dimensional sheet of paper. We have already touched on the subject earlier when we examined the value of working out preliminary details prior to making a half-model. We talked of waterlines which are horizontal slices through the hull, and stations which divide the hull vertically into portions. A glance at a set of lines drawings shows a number of other lines, some straight, others curved, that at first sight seem to really complicate the issue. However, this is not the case.

Drawing Layout

The very essence of a clear set of lines drawings, is the ease with which one can relate a point on the hull in one view, to the equivalent points on the other two views. To that end I would suggest that you adopt a drawing layout with the sheer (profile) plan, showing the side view of the boat, slightly to the left of centre on the paper; the half-breadth plan, which shows the view when looking down from above, directly below; and the body plan, showing the end views of the hull, to the right of the sheer plan and at the same level. On some drawings the body plan may be found superimposed onto the centre station on the sheer plane: this, I feel, can cause the middle of the sheer plan to appear rather jumbled, not to mention a little confusing to anyone not familiar with reading this type of drawing. It may also appear between the sheer plan and the half-breadth plan: this makes it clearer than when it is combined with the sheer plan, but somewhat divorces it from its partners.

Making a Start:
the Waterlines

Now we have established the position of the three views, we can make a start. The first lines to draw are the waterlines which we have already touched on, but more in context to making a half-model rather than a lines drawing.

Start by considering the load-waterline, the level at which the designer intends the boat should float when carrying its normal load of crew, fuel, picnic hamper and perhaps an outboard engine. Calculating exactly where the load-waterline will actually be is quite an involved business and really beyond the scope of this book. For the moment we will simply draw a horizontal line on the paper with enough space above to draw in the hull's topsides, and long enough not only to cater for the length of the boat – to the chosen scale – but also extended far enough to the right to accommodate the body plan as well.

Now draw the remaining waterlines in, above and below, and parallel to the LWL. The distance apart is, perhaps surprisingly, not critical, but for the sake of neatness and to avoid possible mistakes, they are best equally spaced. However, there are exceptions. On many boats, the shape doesn't change a great deal close to the gunwale; below the LWL, however, the width of the hull reduces rapidly as we go deeper. Therefore on some hulls there is a strong argument for having the waterlines closer together below the LWL, and perhaps double-spacing them above.

On the majority of lines drawings the waterlines are numbered, but in a variety of ways. The convention I favour places the LWL as No. 1, then numbers those above the LWL as Nos. 1, 2, 3 … and those below as -1, -2, -3 … . Other drawings may simply have them from No. 1 onwards, starting at the top and working down, and with no special regard for the LWL. Others will be numbered in the reverse direction. The truth is, it doesn't really matter how they are numbered provided they are individually identified.

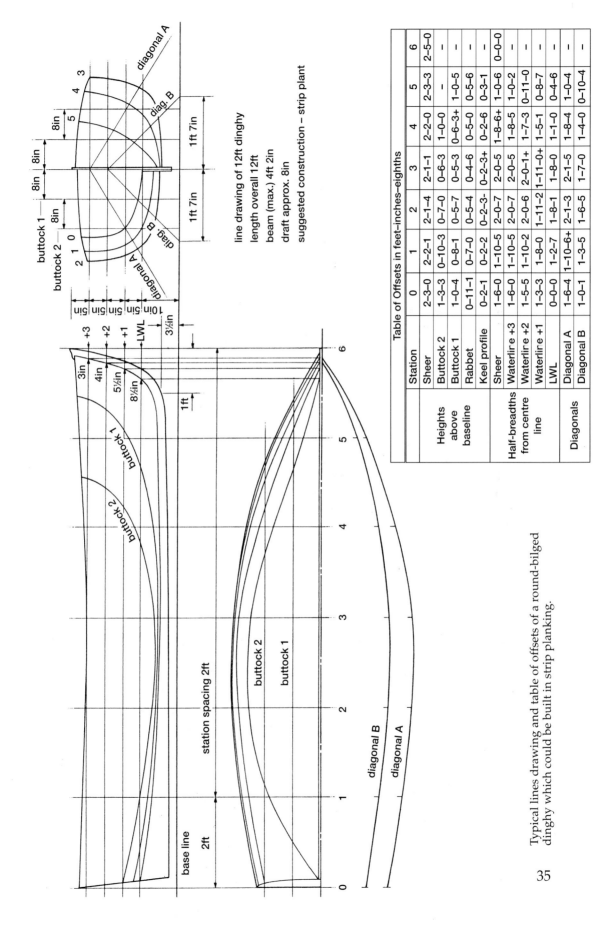

line drawing of 12ft dinghy
length overall 12ft
beam (max.) 4ft 2in
draft approx. 8in
suggested construction – strip plank

Table of Offsets in feet-inches-eighths

	Station	0	1	2	3	4	5	6
Heights above baseline	Sheer	2-3-0	2-2-1	2-1-4	2-1-1	2-2-0	2-3-3	2-5-0
	Buttock 2	1-3-3	0-10-3	0-7-0	0-6-3	1-0-0	–	–
	Buttock 1	1-0-4	0-8-1	0-5-7	0-5-3	0-6-3+	1-0-5	–
	Rabbet	0-11-1	0-7-0	0-5-4	0-4-6	0-5-0	0-5-6	–
	Keel profile	0-2-1	0-2-2	0-2-3-	0-2-3+	0-2-6	0-3-1	–
Half-breadths from centre line	Sheer	1-6-0	1-10-5	2-0-7	2-0-5	1-8-6+	1-0-6	0-0-0
	Waterline +3	1-6-0	1-10-5	2-0-7	2-0-5	1-8-5	1-0-2	–
	Waterline +2	1-5-5	1-10-2	2-0-6	2-0-1+	1-7-3	0-11-0	–
	Waterline +1	1-3-3	1-8-0	1-11-2	1-11-0+	1-5-1	0-8-7	–
	LWL	0-0-0	1-2-7	1-8-1	1-8-0	1-1-0	0-4-6	–
Diagonals	Diagonal A	1-6-4	1-10-6+	2-1-3	2-1-5	1-8-4	1-0-4	–
	Diagonal B	1-0-1	1-3-5	1-6-5	1-7-0	1-4-0	0-10-4	–

Typical lines drawing and table of offsets of a round-bilged dinghy which could be built in strip planking.

35

Drawing the Stations

Next come the stations, or 'sections' as they are sometimes called, on account of them being sectional slices taken across the hull. They appear on the sheer plan as vertical lines, equally spaced, dividing up the overall length of the hull. There is no fixed rule stipulating just how many stations should be included. On small hulls, 2ft (61cm) spacing is about right. Extend the stations down to cover the area of the half-breadth plan. Like the waterlines, the stations should also be numbered. Start at the left of the sheer plan with the rear of the transom, numbering 0, 1, 2, 3, … until the extreme right-hand station is reached.

Completing the Grid

The grid is almost complete, and all that is needed are two centre lines – one for the body plan, the other for the half-breadth plan – and a base line. The two centre lines should be positioned at least half a beam width down from the bottom waterline and the bow station respectively. The base line on a boat of this size can be at the level of the stemhead (top of the stem) parallel with the waterlines, and extended right across both the sheer and body plans. The height above the LWL may be measured off from the half-model.

The next stage is to record faithfully the shape of your half-model or scale model on the grid formed by stations and waterlines. If you have not already done so, draw the stations on the model in the same relative positions as on the plans grid.

Drawing in the Sheer Line

Begin by drawing in the sheer line on the sheer plan, remembering to place the bow facing towards the right. Measure up from the LWL on the model at each station, and draw it in as a point on the equivalent station on the plan. Then with a flexible batten to join up the points, lightly draw in the curve. Use the same technique to draw in the keel line, the transom and the stem/bow transom.

The Rabbet/Rebate

To avoid complicating the issue, I have so far avoided mentioning something called the rabbet or rebate. On a wooden boat, the rabbet (sometimes spelt with two 't's) is the groove cut in the keel, stem and stern post to accommodate the lower edge of the garboard strake – the lowest plank next to the keel – and the hood ends of the planking – the ends of the planks where they attach to the stem and between the end of the keel and the transom. It is therefore this line, rather than the line of the keel and stem, that indicates the bottom of the boat as far as the planking – or the bottom panel in the case of a plywood boat – is concerned. If you are making plans from a half-model without a keel, disregard the rabbet line, otherwise it is the next line to draw onto the sheer plan.

The Half-breadth Plan

Once the basic sheer plan has been completed, attention can be turned to the half-breadth plan and the body plan. First the half-breadth plan, the name of which is a little misleading because it often shows both sides of the hull. But look closely and you will see that both sides are not the same. Both have a series of curves, much like contour lines found on a chart or map. On one side the plan view of the waterlines will be drawn, whilst on the other, the plan view of the diagonals will be projected. If we are looking at the plans of a simple flat-bottomed boat, diagonals are not particularly relevant. On a round-bilged or multi-chine hull, however, they are important – but we will wait until dealing with lofting to investigate them further.

For the moment, therefore, we can limit the half-breadth plan to just one side, and once the outline of the gunwale is drawn in by measuring the half-beam at each station and joining up the points, we must turn our attention towards the body plan which acts very much as a link between the other two views.

The Body Plan

Following convention, draw the view looking from the bow on the right-hand side of the centre line, and the view from astern on the left. If the plans are being drawn to the same scale as the half-model, it would be possible to take a fine saw and cut the models into sections at each station, then simply place the pieces end-on against the centre line and draw the section direct. But I suspect that, having taken the time and care to build their half-models, not many potential boat-builders will be prepared to sacrifice them to the saw; and so we are left with either measuring the sectional shape at each station direct from the model, or making a card template of each station and transposing that onto the body plan. On a round bilge model, the third option is to buy a flexible plastic curve from a drawing supplies shop, and to take off the sections carefully bending it round at each station and recording the result on the body plan, scaling up if necessary.

Drawing in the Co-ordinates

Once the body plan is completed, it is possible to lift off the half-breadth of each waterline at each station and to transfer the dimension directly onto the half-breadth plan. If this is done for each waterline in turn, and the points joined up, it will, on a round-bilged boat, create a series of curves that should be smooth and in sympathy with one another. If they are not, or if they have an unexpected wobble, the problem will be in the hull sections on the body plan, and will indicate that the section where the irregularity exists, needs adjustment. On a flat-bottomed boat, there is little need to project the waterlines down onto the half-breadth plan, but it is certainly worth doing on a multi-chine hull. Although it will not create a smooth curve, it will still show up problems at any of the stations.

The Buttock Lines

There is another set of co-ordinates that we can draw: they too, appear on all three plans and are known as buttock lines. They will help prove the fairness of the hull – again, not really relevant to a flat-bottomed boat, but certainly worth including on all other hull forms.

Very simply, the buttock lines are vertical slices cut parallel to the centre line of the hull and therefore appearing on the half-breadth plan as a series of straight, equally spaced horizontal lines, on the body plan as a series of straight, vertical lines, and on the sheer plan as a set of curves. Like the waterlines projected onto the half-breadth plan, the buttock lines on the sheer plan should appear smoothly curved, gradually coming closer together and then, just as gradually, increasing their spacing as they reach the stern. These lines do not only highlight any irregularities in the hull form, they also provide a good clue as to how the water will flow beneath the hull. At this point, the more plans you study, the better you will appreciate how the different lines relate one to another.

TABLE OF OFFSETS

To those unfamiliar with such things, the table of offsets may seem off-putting – until they take a closer look and discover that the numbers simply relate to everything we have covered in the section on lines drawing. Indeed, the table of offsets is an integral part of the lines drawing and contains the information one needs in order to continue to the next stage. It provides co-ordinates of points around the stations, waterlines and buttock lines relative to the base line and the half-breadth centre line.

The best way of becoming familiar with this form of tables is to examine the example given here, although before you can crack the code completely, you must understand some of the conventions.

Table Layout

First, you must understand the way in which the table is set out. Starting with the left-hand column, at the top is the word 'Stations', and stretching off to the right is 0, 1, 2, 3, 4 ... On some tables you may find the stations specified from left to right as 'Stern, G, F ... A, Bow', depending on the stations' notation on the lines drawing. Provided the two correspond, there is no problem.

Working down the right-hand column, we see that it is divided into two main blocks, both starting with the word 'Sheer'. The top block continues 'Buttock A', 'Buttock B' and so on, whilst the bottom one follows on with the waterlines, progressing downwards towards the keel. The top block of numbers are dimensions

measured from the base line of the sheer and body plans, whilst the one below relates to dimensions taken from the centre line of the half-breadth plan.

On some tables you will find a further set of numbers marked 'diagonals'. Being somewhat controversial, I contend that for small boats of the type we are considering, diagonals tend to complicate the issue and are not really essential. Therefore at this stage we will not pursue their function, but will return to the topic when we are dealing with lofting.

Contemporary designers nearly all work in metric, in which case the dimensions in the squares are all millimetres. But in the days of imperial measurement, dimensions were given in feet and inches, and the dimensions in the squares on a table of offsets were given in feet, inches and eighths of an inch: therefore 2-4-4 would translate into 2ft 4½in (72cm). A convention common to both metric and imperial tables is that all the dimensions are taken to the outside of the planking, the significance of which will become clear in the next chapter.

The Stem Details

Whilst the table of offsets contains virtually all the information provided on a lines drawing, there is one area – sometimes two, depending on hull form – that cannot be reduced to a basic table of numbers, and therefore needs to be included with the table if the whole story is to be told: namely the stem details, which need to be shown separately, especially if the boat has a curved stem. All that is needed is a section of the sheer plan, reproduced with detailed dimensions from the bow station back to both the outside curve of the stem and its rabbet. A glance at the illustration opposite will make this very clear.

Whereas more complex round-bilge hull lines drawings give offset dimensions to points on the waterline, the less complicated shape of a hard-chine hull (flat or vee bottom or multi-chine) usually uses the more direct system of dimensioning to the sheer line and chine(s).

The reason for creating a table of offsets from a lines drawing is to enable us to make a full-size drawing, known as lofting, which we consider a little later. This example follows the old convention of measuring in feet, inches and eighths of an inch. Some modern designs use metric measurements but the basic principle of working from the datum/base line and the half-breadth plan centre line is the same.

	Station	0	1	2	3	4
Dimensions below datum line	Sheer	0-3-7	0-4-6[a]	0-5-1	0-4-3	0
	Chine	1-6-4	1-10-4[b]	1-11-0	1-10-5	1-7-7
Half-breadth from centre line	Sheer	1-5-2	2-0-0[c]	2-1-6	1-7-4	0
	Chine	1-0-5	1-7-5[d]	1-9-1	1-1-7	–

Table of offsets in feet-inches-eighths to outside of planking

letters relate to drawing

Simple line drawing/table of offsets for a 10ft 8in flat-bottom dinghy.

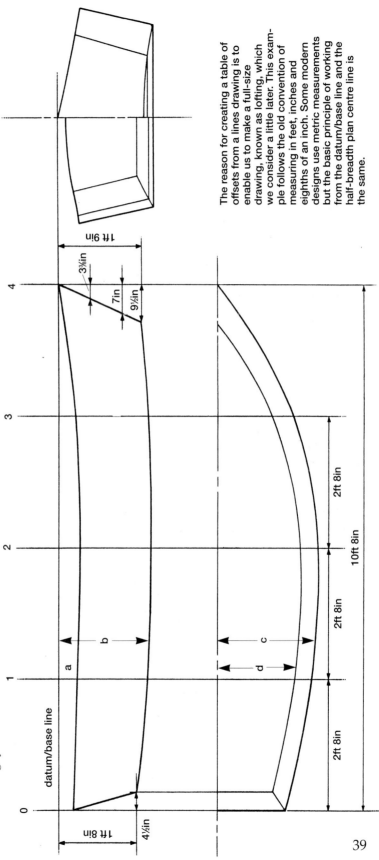

39

MODERN DEVELOPMENTS

Thanks to a number of computer programs, naval architects can produce the lines of a boat and analyse it without the need ever to put pencil to paper. And not only can the program do all the traditional calculations that a designer would have to work out laboriously in long-hand to prove that the boat will float and behave in the way they intend her to, it can also completely build the boat within its memory, working out the shape and size of each individual plank or panel that goes into making the complete hull

By this means, an increasing number of boat designers are able to offer plans that give precise details of how each part of the hull should be cut and shaped, along with a very detailed description of the exact locations and order of assembly. Indeed, so detailed are these plans that the boat can be built without reference to tables of offsets or the need to loft up the design before getting right on with timber and tools. Of course, some types of boat lend themselves more readily to the modern approach which, it cannot be denied, saves a good deal of time and effort. Perhaps the most obvious is the simplest stitch-and-glue construction using plywood panels and woven glass tape and resin to form the seams (a technique we will be discussing later). But even the traditional forms of building such a clinker construction can benefit from computer-aided design in that it can give very reliable details of mould shapes and so on, again without going to the trouble of lofting the design full size. It is even possible to investigate the shape of each individual plank of a clinker hull and produce detailed dimensional drawings so that each plank (strake) could be pre-cut to shape. But just because such programs are available, there is not reason to cast out the old skills.

This is not just a romantic idea of holding onto the past, but a very practical attitude. Having and understanding of the mechanics of lines drawings is perhaps one of the best ways to develop an appreciation of how the shape of a hull evolves, and an eye for a sweet hull. The traditional methods of creating a set of lines drawings is also of particular importance when recording the lines of an existing hull, either as historical interest or as a means of building a replica.

To sum up, there is room for both approaches to boat design. It would be wrong to ignore the traditional approach simply because it gives a short-cut to boat building. But It would be equally wrong to ignore modern techniques which can provide some very valuable answers in a fraction of the time it would take using long-hand methods. And increasingly, these techniques are becoming available to amateur boatbuilders through the services of professional designers, many of whom will happily pick the bones out of an amateur design.

2 Lofting

Lofting is the process of drawing out the lines of a hull, full size. Its purpose is twofold: to sort out any slight dimensional errors, too small to show up on the scale drawings but nevertheless sufficient to spoil the fairness of the hull; and to provide full-size patterns and dimensions necessary for the building of the hull. It is not the black art that some would have you think, but it does seem to present a major hurdle to many prospective boatbuilder. Nevertheless, taken logically, step-by-step, lofting the lines of a small boat should present no real difficulties.

The first problem to solve is to find somewhere suitable to make a full-size drawing. A workshop with a wooden floor, into which you don't mind driving a few spikes and screws, is ideal but if you don't have a wooden floor of sufficient proportions, or are unwilling to sacrifice it to the art of lofting, a very good alternative is ¾in (19mm) thick blockboard. This is extremely cheap compared with plywood, and it usually has a good, smooth surface; it comes in 4 × 8ft sheets. Simply screw as many sheets as you need to create the necessary length onto a couple of battens, paint the surface with a coat of light-coloured emulsion and you have the lofting surface. But don't forget, unless the blockboard is waterproof, it must be kept under cover.

Other equipment you will need is a large wooden tri-square, a steel straight-edge, timber battens of various thicknesses, a handful of fine 2in (50mm) nails, a collection of carpenter's pencils and a chalk-line. This last item is a length of thin string impregnated with chalk-board chalk, used as a guide to drawing long, straight lines. The technique is to stretch it tightly between two nails, then lift it up at the centre by a few inches, and let it ping back onto the floor; in doing so, it will leave a perfectly straight chalk line that can be strengthened and reinforced in pencil, using a straight-edge. You will also need a number of specialist tools, but we will discuss these as their need arises.

MAKING A START

The actual process of lofting is much the same as drawing a lines plan, which we have already covered in some detail, although there are, nevertheless, a number of differences; there is also the task of transferring the lofted drawing onto the timber for frame-making and so on. The three views of the lines drawing are usually superimposed on one another when lofting; this is primarily to save space, but it also avoids unnecessarily duplicating construction lines. And whereas on the scaled-down lines drawing the concentration of lines can cause confusion, there is plenty of room on the full-size lofting to avoid any ambiguity.

At this stage, accuracy is essential and always assume the table of offsets is correct until you prove otherwise.

	Station	0	1	2	3
Heights above baseline	Sheer	2-3-0	2-2-1	2-1-4c	2-1-1
	Buttock 2	1-3-3	0-10-3	0-7-0	0-6-3
	Buttock 1	1-0-4	0-8-1	0-5-7	
	Rabbet	0-11-1	0-7-0	0-5-4d	
	Keel profile	0-2-1	0-2-2	0-2-3e	
Half-breadths from centre line	Sheer	1-6-0a	1-10-5		
	Waterline +3	1-6-0	1-10-5b		
	Waterline +2	1-5-5	1-10-2		
	Waterline +1	1-3-3	1-8-0		
	LWL	0-0-0			
Diagonals	Diagonal A	1-6-4			
	Diagonal B	1-0-1			

letters relate to drawing

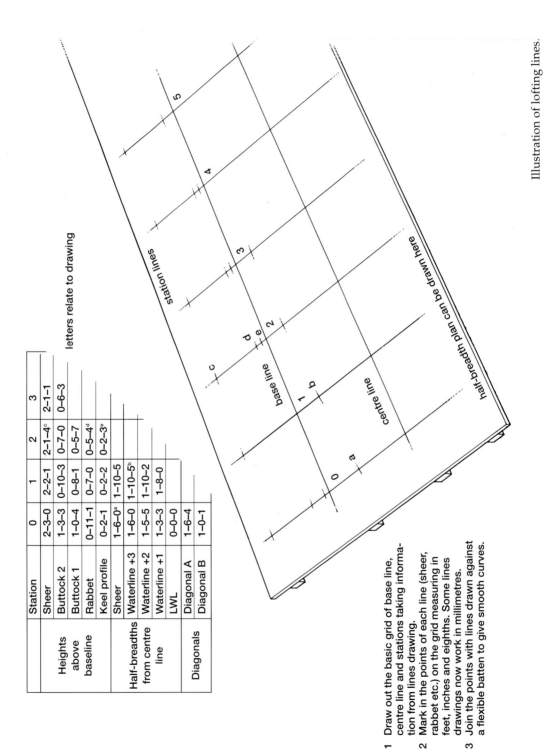

1 Draw out the basic grid of base line, centre line and stations taking information from lines drawing.

2 Mark in the points of each line (sheer, rabbet etc.) on the grid measuring in feet, inches and eighths. Some lines drawings now work in millimetres.

3 Join the points with lines drawn against a flexible batten to give smooth curves.

Illustration of lofting lines.

42

Lofting a Flat-bottomed Craft

We began by building a half-model of a simple flat-bottomed skiff, so for the moment we will consider the straightforward process of lofting such a craft which, although it may not highlight some of the more complex aspects of the art, will provide a worthwhile introduction. We can then fill in the more intricate details once we have gained a basic understanding of the procedure.

Drawing the Sheer Plan

Begin by drawing the base line; unless you have a reliable datum from which to work, this is best done with the chalk-line. Next, lay out a full-size grid of stations and waterlines similar to that used for the sheer plan on the lines drawing; it is then a question of systematically reproducing each line, using the dimensions provided by the table of offsets. Draw in the sheer, bottom, stem and stern lines. In this simplified example we will ignore the keel and rabbet lines, but don't forget to allow for the thickness of the stem. Also, because the boat we are considering at this stage has simple panel sides and a flat bottom, the table of offsets will give dimensions down to the chine line without reference to waterlines.

It is at this point that you discover just how accurately the table of offsets has been drawn up. The lines are drawn in by bending a batten to join up the points drawn at each station. If the curve of the batten suggests that one of the points is not quite in the right place, adjust the

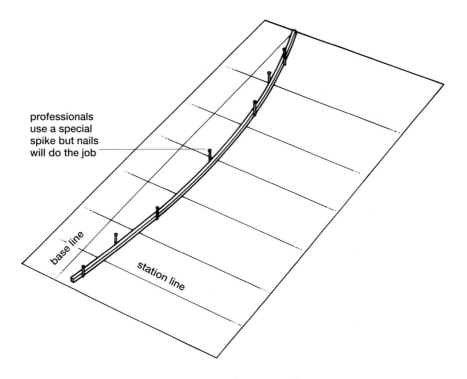

professionals use a special spike but nails will do the job

base line

station line

Drawing in the first lines using a flexible batten to achieve smooth curves.

position of the batten to discover whether the problem is with that particular station, or if it is one of the neighbouring stations that is at fault. If there is no obvious culprit, you then have to decide whether to average out the discrepancy, or simply ignore the point on one station. Usually such problems are easily resolved, but it is a good idea to mark the problem area in case it shows up on another part of the lofting. However, this is not something to worry about unduly, because one of the main purposes of lofting out full size is to show up these discrepancies so you *can* resolve them.

Drawing Up the Half-breadth Plan

Once the basic sheer plan has been completed, it is the turn of the half-breadth plan which is measured in from the half-breadth centre line. Either you can use the waterline to represent the half-breadth centre line, or you can draw in a separate centre line beneath and parallel with the waterlines. It is then again a matter of marking the points of offset at each station for the gunwale and chine lines, once more remembering to allow for the thickness of the stem.

Drawing the Body Plan

Finally we construct the body plan, not from the dimensions given in the table of offsets, but by projecting the heights of the sheer and bottom lines, and by using a marking stick or trammels to transfer the half-breadth offsets directly off the lofted half-breadth plan. For clarity and convenience, use one of the station lines at about the centre of the hull as the centre line. Also follow the same convention as when drawing the lines plans, putting the stern projection to the left of the centre line, and the view from forward of the bow to the right. Joining up the gunwale and chine lines should give smooth, curved lines; if they are not, it is back to the drawing board to discover why. One further step is to project the true shape of the transom which, if angled, is not seen in the body plan. To do this, draw two lines at right-angles to the transom on the sheer plan, then using a marking stick, transfer the transom width from the half-breadth plan.

It is very important to ensure the best possible accuracy, even when lofting a simple design such as this small flat-bottomed skiff. And whilst it is important to reproduce the lines as faithfully as possible from the table of offsets, spot-on accuracy is essential when transferring dimensions from one part of the lofted plan to the other. Many such dimensions will be used directly in the subsequent building of the boat, and if they don't agree on all three projections, the hull simply won't be true.

Lofting Round-Bilged Hull Forms

Before covering the topic of transferring the information from the lofted drawing to frames and moulds, we will take a cursory look at lofting more complicated, round-bilged hull forms. The basics are the same as we have already covered, but in these boats each waterline must be included both to check hull fairness and also to enable the curved sections to be generated. Also, on boats with a more sophisticated hull form, it is common practice to shape the keel to make it wider at the centre of the hull, narrowing towards the stem and stern.

Drawing in the Sheer and Half-breadth Plans

Start by drawing the grid of waterlines and stations measured from a base line. Draw in the basic sheer plan, adding the rabbet round the stem, along the keel and up the stern post to the base of the transom. Draw in a half-breadth centre line, or use the lower waterline as a datum from which to draw the outline of the half-breadth plan, taking the dimensions from the table of offsets. Also, at this stage, draw in the plan view of the keel which, as I have already mentioned, may be wider amidships.

Drawing in the Body Plan and Buttock Lines

Now choose the most convenient station for the centre line of the body plan, and construct the body plan sharing the same waterlines as the sheer plan. Continue until all the station profiles have been drawn, the after sections to the left, the forward sections to the right. We can now make the first check on the fairness of the station profiles by constructing the buttock lines in the sheer plan. These lines are created by taking vertical slices along the hull, at equal intervals parallel to the hull's centre line. On the body plan, therefore, they appear as straight vertical lines equidistant from the centre line. The point at which these lines intersect each station profile is then projected to its equivalent station on the sheer plan.

In our example we have used three buttock lines: each must be projected onto the sheer plan in turn, and the points so produced can be connected using a flexible batten. The aim is to end up with a set of three buttock lines on the sheer plan that are fair and complementary. Any discrepancies should be traced back to the body plan for correction – but not until the next set of co-ordinates has been projected onto the half-breadth plan which will give confirmation of any inaccuracy.

Projecting the Waterlines onto the Half-breadth Plan

When we were considering the preparation of lines drawings, we covered the projection of waterlines onto the half-breadth plan; when lofting, their construction follows exactly the same procedure. Start with the load waterline, measuring the distance from centre line to each station profile on the body plan and transferring the dimensions onto their corresponding stations on the half-breadth plan. Just as before, join up the points on the half-breadth plan stations, and if all is well, it should produce an even curve with the line passing through all the station points. Repeat for all waterlines.

Drawing in the Diagonals

Now for the diagonals, which are much like waterlines but instead of being horizontal, parallel planes, are slices taken longitudinally through the hull, at, or close to 90° to the planking. On the body plan they appear, therefore, as straight lines emanating from the centre line and sloping downwards.

It could be extremely confusing to draw the diagonals on the lofting plan on the same side of the centre line as we used for the half-breadth plan and projected waterlines. If space allowed, we could construct them on the opposite side of the half-body plan; but if this is not a practical proposition draw them using one of the sheer plan waterlines (for convenience,

WL2) to serve as a centre line, with the curves projecting downwards to further avoid confusion.

The first task is to determine the points at the stem and stern where the diagonals start and finish. This is done by simple projection. We will use three diagonals in our example, numbering them from the top: 1a, 1b, 1c, and we will start with 1a. From the bow side of the body plan, draw a horizontal line from the point where the diagonal crosses the rabbet line on the stem, across the corresponding stem rabbet line on the sheer plan. Now drop the line vertically down until it crosses the diagonal's centre line, and measure the distance down diagonal 1a from the body centre line to the point where it crosses the stem rabbet line, i.e. to the point where the first horizontal line was drawn. Transfer the dimension to the diagonal's centre line, measuring down from the centre line along the vertically projected line. That provides the point at which the diagonal starts.

Return to the body plan and do the same for the transom, projecting a line towards the left, this time from the point where the diagonal 1a crosses the transom profile. Carry the line horizontally until it meets the transom on the sheer plan, and then project the line down well beyond the diagonal's centre line. Back to the body plan again, and measure the distance down diagonal 1a from the centre line to the point where it crosses the transom profile. Transfer that dimension to the left-hand vertically projected line from the diagonal's centre line downwards; this point denotes the end of the diagonal at the transom.

From the body plan, measure down the diagonal between the centre line and each station in turn, and transfer the dimensions to their equivalent station on the

half-breadth plan. Using a flexible batten, join the points so created with a pencil line. The curve should be smooth and fair. If it is not, fair up the curve and circle the problem areas for attention later on. Repeat the procedure for the other two diagonals, 1b and 1c.

CORRECTING THE BODY PLAN

If you have been working from a very accurately prepared table of offsets and have been incredibly lucky, the waterlines, buttock and diagonal fairing lines will all turned out beautifully smooth with no kinks or hollows. If this is the case, you can move on to the final stages of lofting. The chances are, however, that you will have highlighted one or two places where the fared line and the measured point didn't agree. This may seem disheartening, but it does serve to demonstrate the importance of lofting: many a boat has been built without being fully lofted, only for the builder to discover that somewhere along the line, someone has made a small error at the design stage, an error which lofting would have pinpointed easily, but which without lofting went undiscovered until it was too late to correct.

It is not too difficult to isolate the problem area on a lofted plan. To put things right, the profile of the offending station on the body plan must be changed to agree with the fair waterline, buttock or diagonal line. The problem is that the three fairing lines are interdependent, and if it is necessary to correct a station profile for one, the other two will probably also show a problem. Moreover, having once changed the profile on one of the body plan stations to make it correspond with one of the fairing lines, it may well be necessary to re-check it out against its two companion lines. It may seem as if one is going round in circles at this point, but a little patience can save a great deal of frustration and disappointment later on. There are really no hard-and-fast rules as to the best way to achieve a fair hull; it is a matter of working methodically.

PLANK THICKNESS

It is merely convention that the lines offsets are taken to the outside of the hull. This means that before the boatbuilder can take up his tools, the thickness of the planking must be superimposed onto the lofted body plan. If the boat is to be built of plywood, either in panels or for laminates when cold moulding, deciding on plank thickness is simple. Where the plans call for the boat to be planked in ¼in (6mm) ply, that is what you allow. But there are exceptions, and carvel planked using solid timber is the most obvious. Some of the thickness of the plank may well be lost due to fairing the outside of the hull. Also, don't make the mistake of simply reducing the width of the frames by the thickness of the planking (plywood skin) because that would not give an accurate result – draw it out, this will soon become clear.

Once you have settled on the final plank thickness, work your way round each station profile using either a pencil compass or a marking template to create parallel lines representing the inside of the planking. On single and multi-chine hulls, this will mean just two marks per panel, to be joined using a straight-edge. The body plan of a round-bilged hull, on the other hand, should be marked every 4 to 5in (10 to 12.7cm) so that an accurate inner line can be drawn using a flexible batten to join the points. This is a time when you will definitely need more than one pair of hands, but with strategically placed nails and a few small sandbags, it is surprising what the lone lofter can achieve.

At this stage it is easy to forget that the boat you are building may have a deck. Just as the lines plans are drawn to the outside of the planking, they also include the thickness of any decking. Again, this may seem a minor point for the newcomer to boat building, but it could be very significant when possibly building more adventurous craft later on.

TRANSFERRING THE LINES

Although the inexperienced builder will glean a great deal of information from a lofted design, the main purpose behind the exercise, as far as the less seasoned builder is concerned, is to produce a set of building moulds and frames over which the hull can be both accurately and symmetrically constructed. Transferring the body plan sections by measurement would simply not be accurate enough, and would provide too great an opportunity for mistakes. It is much better to transfer the shapes of the stations by more direct means. Traditionally, boatbuilders do this using copper tacks pressed sideways into the lofting floor along the station profile, so that half the head of each tack is left proud and aligned with the curve representing the inside of the planking. The oversize mould blank can then be carefully positioned over the tacks so that the heads puncture the surface of the mould, faithfully reproducing the lofted curve in a series of marks.

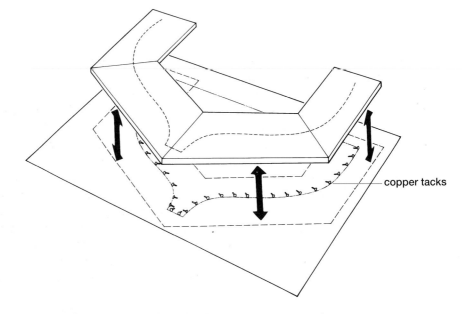

copper tacks

Transferring section shapes by pressing the timber frames over copper tacks marking the lines. This method is really only needed when building round bilge hulls.

Stage 1 Align the front ends of the marking blocks with the outline drawn on the lofting board using a square. Then either fasten the blocks in place or draw location marks on the board, around the marking blocks.

Stage 2 Slip the roughly shaped mould beneath the marking blocks and transfer the outline of the frame to the mould.

Stage 3 Mark the position of each marking block face on the mould then connect the points using a flexible batten to produce a smooth curve.

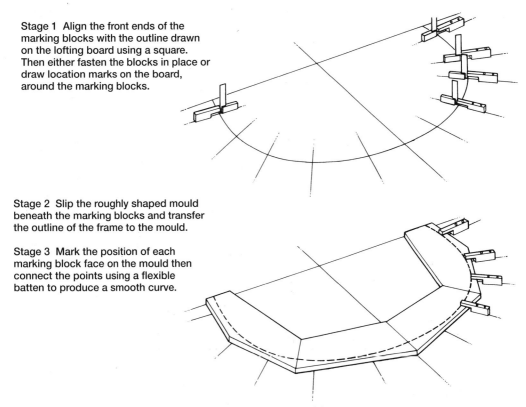

Transferring the lofted shape of a frame onto a timber mould.

Alternatively, the profile can be reproduced using batten guides – stepped pieces of timber, the ends of which are first positioned over the line to be reproduced, nailed or screwed in place, and then the frame or mould blank slipped in place under the steps. A batten is then bent around the ends of the batten guides to reproduce the curve on the blank. The batten can be held in place by driving nails adjacent to the ends of the guides.

It is possible to trace the shapes of small items onto tracing paper, and then to transfer the drawing directly onto the timber. But this method is not really suitable for recreating the profiles of full frames or moulds because paper is notoriously unstable; it is surprising just how much a large sheet can change size with a change of humidity.

TAKING LINES

Most wooden boat enthusiasts probably spend at least some spare moments poking about in an old-fashioned boatyards and foreshores where old wooden boats are left to end their days. Many of these ancient hulls are worthy cases for recording, and a technique very similar to lofting can be used to lift off the lines and put them on paper either with a view to building a boat similar in style, or simply for posterity so that one day, others will have the opportunity to bring these traditional craft back to life.

To do this, the hull must first be chocked up and levelled, bringing the load-waterline as near horizontal as possible. Check along the boat's length with a spirit level to ensure that any twist that has set in over the years is taken out by diagonally propping her

The shape of the hull section can be taken at intervals along the length of the hull to build up a picture that can be transferred to a flat board.

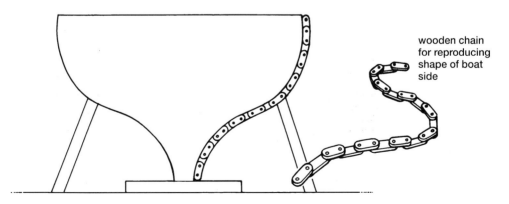

wooden chain for reproducing shape of boat side

Taking the lines off an existing hull.

beneath the gunwale. If taking the lines from a small dinghy or workboat, it could be more convenient to take the measurements with the hull upside-down, supporting the craft beneath the gunwale, and again ensuring the hull has any twist taken out.

Before measuring can begin, you need a datum from which to measure. This can take the form of a simple frame bridging the hull, on which the positions of the waterlines are marked on one or both legs.

Divide the length of the hull into a convenient number of equally spaced stations, and erect the frame at each station in turn. Measure from the leg of the frame, horizontally to the hull planking at each waterline. When all the dimensions have been recorded, they can be set out to provide a table of offsets. The shape of the

stem can be measured by taking dimensions from a straight-edge set perpendicularly against the stemhead.

Alternatively a photograph can be taken, using a standard lens (50mm on a 35mm camera) and positioned so that the lens is about half-way up the stem and at sufficient distance almost to fill the frame. Avoid using a wide-angle lens because this can create distortion. Use a good-size enlargement and scale the dimensions directly off the print. The same technique can be employed to check the transom shape. However, the profile of the sheer plan cannot be scaled successfully from a photographic print because of distortion. But it is always useful, when taking the lines of a hull, to take a good selection of photographs to record design details.

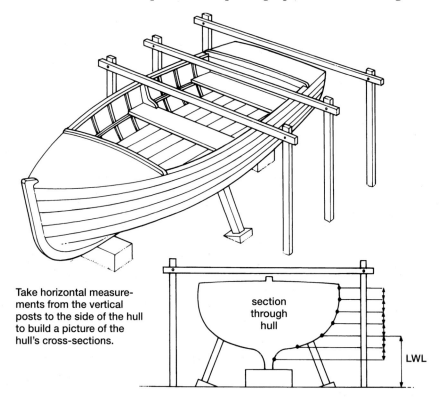

Take horizontal measurements from the vertical posts to the side of the hull to build a picture of the hull's cross-sections.

section through hull

LWL

Taking the lines off a hull by measurement.

3 Tools and Materials

TOOLS OF THE TRADE

Never go out and buy tools unless and until they become absolutely necessary to the job you have in hand. For that reason alone, never invest in toolsets: invariably much of the cost goes on a fancy box, and even more on odd size tools that you will never need. There will, of course, be exceptions, and it would be a mistake to forego a bargain. But before you part with hard-earned cash, be certain you can't do the job without it. Nevertheless a boatbuilder's toolchest should contain the basic woodworking tools. But buy them as you need them: that way you know exactly what you are looking for, and that the tool will exactly suit the particular job in hand.

Sadly, the golden age of good quality hand tools, and especially woodworking tools, is past. It is not that you can no longer get the steel, but cheap, substandard tools have flooded the market. Thankfully, however, good quality tools have not disappeared altogether, and even though costly, they are worth their price and easily earn their keep in a short time. The main point about buying good quality cutting tools is that they can be brought to a high state of sharpness, and they stay that way for longer. And sharp tools are perhaps the most important factor in achieving a good result.

Although I have advised against buying sets of hand tools, in my opinion the bare minimum to have is four bevelled-edged chisels ranging in size from ⅛in (3mm) to 1½in (37mm) wide, a smoothing plane, tenon and ripsaws, a tri-square, screwdrivers and hammers. The adjustable bevel must also be placed on the list of essential tools, even though slightly more specialized. And you can never have too many clamps – although here again, it is important to buy the right design, and you can only find out which you like working with best by trial and, we hope, not too much error.

Now, although there are exceptions, the quality of a tool is directly proportional to its price. And there is little doubt that the better the tool, the easier it is to use, and the better will be the result. The old adage about the bad workman blaming his tools may hold a lot of truth, but a bad tool will make a bad workman out of anyone. The two features to look for are quality of construction and the ability to retain a sharp edge. A plane, for instance, should look and feel solid and well finished; likewise a chisel should have a fine finish, and should not look as if it has been ground to shape on a millstone. It is very difficult for the inexperienced to tell if a blade will stay sharp. The best policy is to buy only reputable names, although with experience, the newcomer to woodworking will develop an instinct not only for what looks right in a blade, but also for what feels right. In a nutshell, buy the best quality you can afford, and never forget that the most expensive tool is the one that you have to discard because it doesn't do the job you want of it.

ELECTRIC HAND TOOLS

Because the amateur boatbuilder does not charge for his or her time, electrically powered hand tools are not strictly necessary. However, there are situations where a little motive force is very welcome. For example the electric hand planer, of which there are a whole range on the market, saves a lot of hard work, and could also represent a considerable financial saving. Like so many tools, it should be used with the utmost respect because, if handled carelessly, it could inflict a terrible injury on you, and do a great deal of damage to your surroundings. But properly used, it will enable you to convert rough, sawn timber to the boards you want, and this represents a significant saving on cost compared with buying prepared timber. Of course, it has its limits, and although I'm sure it is possible to plane wide boards successfully, the best results are obtained with timber which is just a single width of the cutter.

Another electric tool which I think is worth its keep is a portable jigsaw. In my experience, it does not replace conventional hand saws, for which there will always be a need, but for cutting out panels from large sheets of plywood, it has no equal as far as the amateur is concerned.

There was a time when I could drive in a gross of screws without the slightest sign of a blister on the palm of my right hand. This is no longer the case, and my hand has become soft thanks to that most labour-saving of tools, the electric screwdriver. In its most basic form, driving

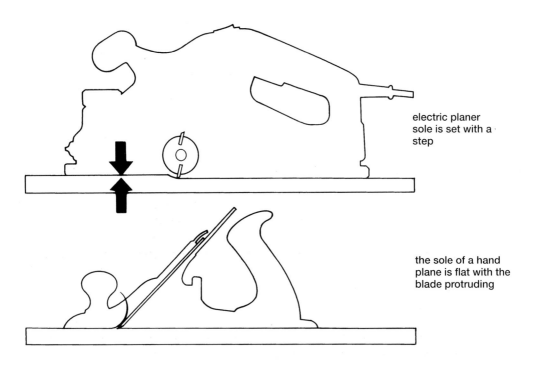

electric planer sole is set with a step

the sole of a hand plane is flat with the blade protruding

It is important to understand the difference between the setting of an electric planer and a hand plane.

screws is all it will do – but for a few pounds more you can have a versatile rechargeable drill that not only drills the holes but drives the screws with effortless ease; until, that is, the battery needs recharging. So, for another few pounds you can purchase a rechargeable electric drill with an interchangeable battery, so that whilst one is powering the drill, the other battery can be quietly replenishing. Certainly this is one of the few electric tools that I would be loath to give up.

TIMBER

Since the advent of glass-reinforced plastics (GRP), wood has received some very negative press, it has often been suggested that a timber-built boat is nothing but a labour of love needing constant repainting and hours of tedious maintenance. However, if timber were to be discovered today, it would undoubtedly be heralded as the new wonder material ideally suited for building boats: light, easily worked, flexible, with a high strength-to-weight ratio … the list goes on.

But those who have ever visited a timberyard with the intention of buying timber will have experienced the rather disconcerting secret language they use: 'sawn or par, and is that nominal? And watch out for the shakes.' Some of those who are 'in the know' seem to delight in trying to confuse those who are not – but the answer to this is simple: choose your supplier carefully. There are timberyards that specialize in supplying boatbuilders, and these are well worth supporting. Local timberyards are also worth investigating, although it is a good idea to telephone ahead; they often use potentially dangerous machinery and so understandably do not like people wandering in unannounced. Also, many are not set up to supply small quantities of timber, nor are they willing to do so, and a pre-emptive call can save disappointment. However, you could ask if they supply any stockists local to your area; it is often possible to order your timber through a local yard and actually purchase it more cheaply than if you had gone direct to the big timber importer.

It is also well worth taking the time to learn just some of the language of timber, and to know precisely what you are looking for in terms of size and quantity. First, size: most timberyards have now been dragged reluctantly into the metric age, although they still regard the old imperial measurement system with fondness. The area where metrication has really taken hold is in standard lengths, and to the layman, logic seems to have very little to do with it: it is hard to understand why 1.8m and 2.1m are standard lengths in many timberyards, whilst 2m is not. The best course to adopt is simply to tell them exactly what you want.

So, if you are buying from a yard that still cuts to your list, don't try to work out what you think are the most economical sizes: simply present your cutting list, and the person at the yard will be able to tell you exactly what to buy. On the other hand, if you are dealing with an establishment that just sells a range of pre-cut sizes, then you will have to calculate whether it is more economical to buy a plank and saw it to the size you require, or to buy it ready-machined to size.

A great deal of confusion can result from the two simple words used in timberyard parlance: 'nominal' and 'finished'. The traditional way of measuring timber was at the sawn stage, before it was made beautifully smooth by planing; as a rough guide, about ⅛in (3mm) is removed from both the thickness and the width when the timber passes through a planer. The nominal size, therefore, is the size to which the timber is sawn, whilst the **finished size** is somewhat smaller. For example, if you insisted that your timber ended up exactly 1in (25mm) thick, most timberyards will oblige, but only by machining down from thicker timber for which the customer must pay.

The expression 'par' means 'planed all round'; it is also known as 'prepared' timber. It is very convenient to buy timber in this way, but you certainly have to pay for the facility. A far more economical alternative is to buy the timber in the sawn state, and to prepare it yourself using an electric hand planer. Wider planks are not so easy for the amateur to handle in this way, but it is worth investigating how much a local joinery firm would charge to run the wood through their planer before making a final decision on whether to buy the timber sawn or prepared.

CHOOSING TIMBER

If you are buying timber from a supplier who specializes in servicing boatbuilders, you may feel confident simply to specify what you intend using it for, and to rely on their experience and integrity to supply the right stuff. But not all timberyard personnel know what the boatbuilder really wants, and to deal with those situations you need a few more answers.

Methods of Sawing

First, you should understand the way in which the log is sawn. When sawing planks from a log, the sawyer has to decide whether to plain-saw, which is sometimes referred to as fletch-cutting, or to quarter-saw. As far as the timberyard is concerned, the difference is that plain-sawing is both quicker and less wasteful. A plain-sawn log is simply cut into layers, in a way that takes no account of how the grain runs across each plank. Quarter-sawing, on the other hand, aligns the planks so that the growth rings run across the thickness of each plank rather than along the width. True quarter-sawing is quite wasteful because it means that the log is cut with the planks radiating from the centre like radial spokes of a wheel, and it is easy to see that this is not really compatible with parallel thickness planks. There is, however, a compromise known as modern quarter-sawing, which results in almost the same quantity of cut but produces fewer planks that will have a tendency towards warping. The important thing to remember is that changes in moisture content will cause the growth rings to straighten. (We will look at the effects of changing moisture content a little later.)

Stability is not the only reason for quarter-sawing: the appearance of the timber can often be dramatically changed. Perhaps one of the best examples of this is with Douglas fir, where one face will show narrowly spaced, straight, contrasting lines, whilst the adjacent surface will exhibit a far less dense, rounded grain pattern.

The problem for the amateur builder is that of scale. The professional boatbuilder will probably buy the whole log, and can therefore specify the way in which it is to be cut. The amateur is likely to need only a fraction of the log, and so will have to accept what is offered. But if you explain to the timberyard people that you are building a boat, most will be willing to help select planks that are suitable.

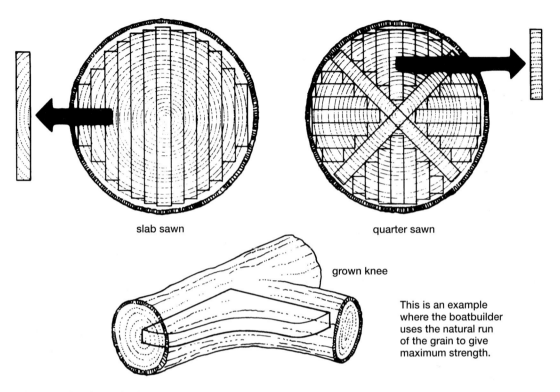

slab sawn

quarter sawn

grown knee

This is an example where the boatbuilder uses the natural run of the grain to give maximum strength.

(*Above*) Timber from the log.

(*Below*) The effect of different directions of sawing.

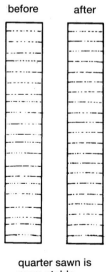

before   after

quarter sawn is more stable

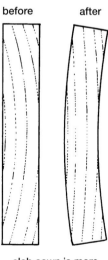

before   after

slab sawn is more likely to curl

Seasoning

During seasoning the moisture content of a tree is encouraged to fall by drying to a point where it is in equilibrium with the moisture content in the surrounding atmosphere. This can be achieved in one of two ways: either the timber can be left 'in stick' to dry naturally; or it can be artificially dried, a process known a 'kiln drying'. Many boatbuilders prefer the former natural approach because natural seasoning – which takes around a year per 1in (25mm) of thickness – also allows time for the timber to relax. Many believe that kiln-drying can encourage pent up stress which shows up when the timber is subsequently machined. Another problem that can occur with kiln-dried timber is cracking, which is usually a sign that the process has not been sufficiently controlled. But provided the timber has been properly kiln-dried, there is no reason why it shouldn't be used for boat building.

For most boat-building purposes, the timber needs to be properly seasoned. The exception is oak for steam-bent timbers (ribs) in the construction of traditional clinker and carvel hulls. Such timber needs to be bought green, that is, unseasoned.

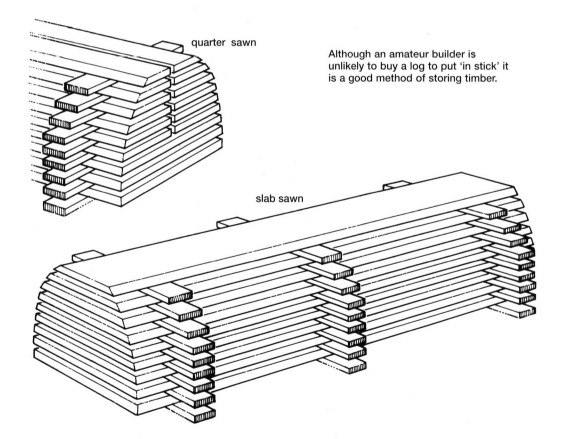

quarter sawn

slab sawn

Although an amateur builder is unlikely to buy a log to put 'in stick' it is a good method of storing timber.

Traditional way of seasoning timber 'in stick'.

Seasoning is the job of the timberyard merchant who can normally be relied upon to deliver fully seasoned timber, especially if the purpose is made clear at the time of ordering. However, yards that specialize in supplying the building trade hold stocks of timber that often has a far higher moisture content than is desirable for boat building. Nevertheless, if they have the quality you want, and the price is right, it may be worth continuing the seasoning process at home. This is achieved by stacking the boards in a dry, unheated place such as a garage. It must be done in such a way as to allow air to circulate through the stack, by spacing the boards apart from each other with narrow sticks of wood (hence the expression 'in stick') for a reasonable period of time. If you have the use of a moisture meter, you will be looking for a 15 per cent moisture content.

Assuming that the seasoning has been completed either by the supplier, or in the garage at home, the timber will be in a relatively stable condition. But if it has been stored in the open or in a damp shed, then the moisture content might have increased and this could cause problems when it is brought into a dry workshop, allow plenty of time for conditions to equalize.

Durability

A final consideration, apart from selecting the actual species of timber for a particular job, is to look at its durability, and exactly what durability means in the timber world. A specific test was formulated by the British Timber Research and Development Association which involves driving a 2×2in (50×50mm) stake into the ground. The stake should be of heart timber, properly seasoned and untreated. In those extreme conditions, a 'perishable' timber will rot in less than five years; 'non-durable' timber would rot away in five to ten years; 'moderately durable' species in ten to fifteen years; 'durable' timber in fifteen to twenty-five years, whilst 'very durable' timber takes more than twenty-five years to rot.

The generally accepted rule is that timbers suitable for the marine environment should be at least moderately durable. But there are exceptions, although care has to be taken as to where in the hull they are used. Rock elm is a case in point: it is classed as non-durable, but it certainly has its place in boat building. Moreover, as some traditionally used species become more difficult to obtain in the sizes and quality needed for boat building, we may well see a move towards the use of less durable timbers, especially in the more traditional forms of construction, in conjunction with chemical timber preservatives. Certainly we are going to be forced by circumstance, if not by legislation, into using sustainable species that are perhaps not so attractive but which do an adequate job, and the cropping of which does not represent a threat to our environment. The following section lists some of the more common boat-building timbers.

Afromosia (Pericopsis elata)

A yellow/brown hardwood with brown markings, used for keels, hogs, deadwoods and other areas where toughness and durability are important factors. Although moderately hard, it is easy to work. It finishes smoothly with a fine even texture and a fine interlocking grain. It tends to split when nailed, but polishes and glues well. Very stable and extremely durable, but it stains when in contact with steel It weighs 43lb/ft³ (688kg/3m³). Also known as kokrudua.

NOTE: Some yards refuse to deal in afromosia because it is listed in Appendix 11, *Timber Species Controlled Under The Convention of International Trade In Endangered Species* (CITES), and EU Directives. This covers species which may become threatened if trade is not controlled. Companies trading in this timber must have permits from both the country of origin and the DoE. Therefore it can be difficult to obtain.

Agba (Gossweilerodendron balsamiferum)

Light brown or pinkish-brown and classed as durable/moderately durable, this hardwood is a versatile timber used for planking, decking and such-like. It nails and glues well. It bleaches lighter than teak and weighs 32lb/ft³ (512kg/m³). Also known as tola.

Ash, European (Fraxinus excelsior)

White with a possible pink hue, this hardwood is used for jib-booms, tillers, cleats and boathook shafts. This is a perishable timber but it works easily, and glues and finishes well. It also takes polish and stain well, and has a rather medium/coarse texture. Excellent bending characteristics. Weight 43lb/ft³ (688kg/m³).

Cedar, Western Red (Thuya plicata)

Classed as very durable, this reddish-brown softwood is an excellent lightweight timber used almost exclusively for strip planking and cold-moulding, for which special sections and veneers are produced. It nails and glues reasonably well, and is easy to work and finish. It weighs 24lb/ft³ (385kg/m³). The dust it produces when worked can be an irritant.

Elm, Rock (Ulmus thomasi)

A pale brown hardwood used mainly for frames and rubbing strakes. It is classed as moderately durable, and is strong and elastic. It screws, nails and glues satisfactorily; it also finishes smooth, and varnishes and paints well. Weight: 44lb/ft³ (704kg/m³). It should not be confused with American white elm or swamp elm.

Elm, Wych (Ulmus glabra)

A matt brown timber (British) used for transoms and rubbing strakes. It screws and nails well, is fairly easy to work, and it finishes well. It is classed as non-durable, and is particularly susceptible to rot in fresh water. Weight 42lb/ft³ (672kg/m³).

Fir, Douglas (Pseudotsuga menziesii)

A light reddish-brown softwood with a medium texture and marked flame-like grain. It is moderately durable, and used for fitting out, planking, thwarts and spars. Weight 33lb/ft³ (530kg/m³).

Iroko (Clorophora excelas)

A yellow-brown hardwood that darkens with age and is used as an alternative for teak. It is classed as durable to very durable, and is moderately easy to work. It screws, nails and glues satisfactorily, and finishes well. Its irregular grain may cause distortion, although it is otherwise stable. Weight 40lb/ft³ (640kg/m³).

Keruing *(Dipterocarpus)*

A hardwood with a range of colour from pinkish-brown right through to dark brown. It is used for structural work and unpainted decks, and is moderately durable with a coarse and even texture. Weight 42 to 51lb/ft³ (810kg/m³). It is also known as apitong, gurjun or lang.

Larch, European (Larix decidua)

A pale reddish softwood with a fine texture. It is moderately durable to non-durable, and can be resinous. Used for planking, masts and spars and decking, it is a stable timber which screws, nails and glues well. It weighs 34lb/ft³ (550kg/m³).

Mahogany, African (Khaya *spp)*

A reddy-brown colour which darkens on weathering, this is a moderately durable hardwood used generally throughout boat building, for planking, bulkheads, transoms and general fitting out. It is slightly less dense than the American species, and can be a little difficult to work thanks to its interlocking grain. However, it finishes well, and also screws, nails and glues well, and it is stable. It weighs 35lb/ft³ (560kg/m³).

Mahogany, American-Honduras (Swietenia macrophylla)

This is a light reddy-brown to straw-coloured hardwood classed as durable and used generally for boat building, though especially favoured for planking. It is easy to work, it screws, nails and glues satisfactorily, and it can be brought to a high finish. It weighs 34lb/ft³ (544kg/m³). Its sources include Brazil, and although the supply is strictly controlled and licensed, there is currently a good deal of controversy over its use; it should therefore only be purchased from reputable suppliers.

Makore (Tieghemella heckalii)

A dark reddy-brown to pinkish-coloured West African hardwood: it is very durable and is used for planking. It screws, nails and glues well, but although it can be worked moderately easily to a fine finish, it can dull tools. Moreover, when worked, it produces a fine dust and this can be an irritant. It weighs 39lb/ft³ (624kg/m³).

Oak, Japanese (Quercus mongolica)

A pale yellow, moderately durable hardwood used for keels, hogs, deadwoods, frames, timbers (when green) knees and breasthooks. It nails and glues and bends well, with a medium texture, but it strains when in contact with steel. Weight: 42lb/ft³ (670kg/m³).

Oak, American White (Quercus *spp)*

A pale yellow to reddish-brown hardwood used for keels, stems, deadwoods, frames, timbers, stringers, knees and breasthooks. It is usually straight-grained, but it can have a coarse and uneven texture which makes it difficult to work; otherwise it works moderately well. It is very strong and hard, and classed as moderately durable to durable; it is also extremely resistant to water. It screws, nails and glues well, but if it comes into contact with damp iron, it will stain. It weighs 48lb/ft³ (770kg/m³).

Pine, Pitch *(Pinus palustris)*

A yellow-brown to reddish-brown, moderately durable softwood with medium stability, used mainly for planking. It is hard and strong, but a little difficult to finish due to its resinous nature. It is also moderately difficult to nail and screw. It weighs 41lb/ft³ (655kg/m³). An excellent boat-building timber, but sadly now quite difficult to obtain.

Redwood, European *(Pinus sylvestris)*

Pale reddy-brown to yellow-brown, moderately durable softwood used mainly for planking, thwarts and floorboards. It is easy to work, nail and screw, and it glues well. It also varnishes and paints satisfactorily. Weight: 31lb/ft³ (496kg/m³).

Spruce, Sitka *(Picea sitchensis)*

A light pinkish-brown softwood with a high sheen, used for canoe planking, oars, paddles, masts and spars. This is a non-durable species but its beauty and light weight make it a favourite of spar-makers. It works, nails, screws and glues well. Its weight is 28lb/ft³ (448kg/m³).

Teak *(Tectona grandis)*

Perhaps the best known of all boat building timbers, teak is medium- to golden-brown, straight grained, very durable and mainly used for decking and planking. It

screws, nails and glues well, but it may split if it is nailed too near to an edge. Weight: 41lb/ft³ (656kg/m³).

Utile *(Entandrophragma utile)*

A purple to reddy-brown durable hardwood used mainly for carlins, coamings and planking. It has a striped grain and is fairly stable. It works fairly well, but it will dull cutting tools. It also nails, screws and glues satisfactorily. Weight: 41lb/ft³ (660kg/m³).

CHOOSING PLYWOOD

Increasingly, plywood is being used in the construction of traditional-style designs where building in solid timber has become extremely expensive or there are difficulties in finding the right quality of timber for planking. Plywood construction also lends itself to the use of modern adhesives, which we will deal with later.

There are four types of plywood that may be offered for boat building: they are moisture-resistant (MR); boil-resistant (BR); weather- and boil-proof (WBP) and marine plywood (MP). Moisture-resistant plywood is not suitable for building hulls, but can be used where it will not come into direct contact with water, which is very limiting on a small boat. Boil-resistant comes closer, but WBP is the obvious choice for hull construction. The glues used in the manufacture of the plywood should conform to BS 1203:1979, or in the case of proper marine plywood, BS 1088:1966. The one to avoid is labelled 'resin-bonded' with no further qualification.

That is the rough guide, but you still have to be very careful. There are imported plywoods currently on the market that are clearly not what their markings claim they are. Genuine marine plywoods have clear faces which should be without defects or gaps in either the face or the core veneers. The inside veneers should also be of a durable timber, and of the same quality as the face veneers, and there should be no natural defects or any sapwood. Genuine BS 1088 marine plywood must be glued with a weather-and-boil-proof adhesive which will most likely be phenol formaldehyde glue (urea formaldehyde glue is commonly used in exterior grade plywood). This is resistant to attack from cold and boiling water, steam and dry heat, and micro-organisms.

Traditionally, the best check to show that what you have is genuine marine plywood has been the British Standards Kitemark, but there are currently very few brands that carry this mark. Another mark to look for is Lloyd's Approval. However, be cautious of the label that claims manufacture to 'Lloyd's standards': such claims are worthless unless they are backed up by actual certification. The bottom line is that you are very much in the hands of the supplier.

Like marine plywood, exterior grade plywood is available in a range of qualities, depending on source, species and country of origin. If you are careful and know what to look out for, exterior grade plywoods can be found that are perfectly satisfactory for building small boats, and which are somewhat cheaper than the same thickness marine plywood. The points to watch out for are these: the number and size of gaps in the core veneers, sometimes difficult to spot without cutting the sheet; and both the quality and the thickness of the veneers, especially the face veneers which are unlikely to be of equal thickness to the core veneers but should not be paper thin. The problems with thin outer veneers are as follows: possible weakness in one direction; splitting and splintering of the surface when sawn; and they cannot be sanded without a high risk of sanding through to the glue line.

Like many things relating to the timber trade, the specification of size and thickness can be a little confusing. Thickness is now almost universally specified in millimetres, but sheet size is still sometimes referred to in old-fashioned feet. The basic size is 8ft by 4ft (2.4m by 1.2m), and it is invariably the most economical size to buy. However, some suppliers will subdivide sheets into 8ft by 2ft (2.4m by 0.6m). Some specialist companies can supply sheets 12ft (3.6m) long, whilst others offer a scarfing service for those who require 16ft (34.8m) or even 24ft (61m) long sheets. It is important to remember when both planning panel layout and ordering plywood, that the surface veneer grain always runs in the direction of the first dimension. Although when sold in metric sheet sizes, the millimetres are usually a direct conversion from the standard 8ft by 4ft (2.4m by 1.2m) dimensions, metric sheets are sometimes significantly larger than their imperial counterparts. The extra is not always welcome, especially when dimensions on plans are given from both ends of the sheet, so it is a wise precaution to run a tape measure over the panel before marking it out, and also to check it for squareness.

Standard thicknesses range from 1in to ³⁄₁₆in (25mm to 4mm) and all have an uneven number of veneers which are usually arranged at right-angles to one another. There are, however, exceptions where the veneers are deliberately arranged to give increased strength in one direction for making such things as centreboards and rudder blades.

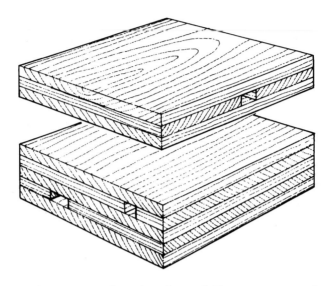

Examples of gaps in internal veneers in sub-quality plywood. These are sources of weakness and should be avoided.

The most common grades of surface finish are 'good two sides' and 'good one side'. The former is really only necessary if it is to be varnished on both sides, and the latter is often significantly cheaper without undue reduction in overall quality.

Plywood comes in a whole range of timber species and sources of manufacture. The following section gives a simplified summary of those most commonly used in boat building.

Exterior Grade (WBP) Plywood

Baltic Pine

High in quality and light in weight, Baltic pine plywood needs only light preparation to produce a good, clean finish. However, it is sometimes manufactured with non-durable, softwood cores. It is best suited for fitting out and panelling where lightness is an important factor. It is relatively expensive.

Birch, Finnish

Birch is a non-durable timber which should not be used in contact with water. However, it can be used effectively in conjunction with glass-epoxy sheathings, in which case it can be used in exposed areas. It has a dense, high quality face veneer which is white to cream in colour. Birch plywood has the occasional plug in the face veneer where a knot has been removed, making it more suited to being finished in paint rather than varnish. Certainly a good board for fitting-out work where a smooth, good quality finish is required, and relatively inexpensive.

Douglas Fir

A moderately durable softwood board which is light brown in colour. Available in a wide range of quality from 'clean finish' boards perfectly suitable for boat building, down to the lowest grades used on building sites which unfortunately is the end of the market that many suppliers concentrate on – so choose carefully. Douglas fir is a timber that has increased in price in recent years, but it is reliable, and it is very good used in conjunction with epoxy resin and glass sheathing in the construction of hulls.

Plywoods from the Far East

Often having the appearance of mahogany, this type of plywood is not identified by species, but can range in colour from red right through the shades to white. The core veneers are often subject to gaps and the faces may be subject to discoloration and plugs, but it is usually manufactured from a durable timber. It is also usually very well priced, but you must choose extremely carefully if it is intended for building a hull. It is best reserved for internal fitting out.

Teak-faced Plywood

Although teak is synonymous with boat building, teak-faced plywood is not really considered as a viable board for building hulls, mainly due to its high cost. It is just one of a whole range of plywoods produced with exotic hardwood veneers and, as such, is usually limited to high-class interior fitting-out on yachts.

Marine Plywoods, BS 1088

Gaboon

This plywood is an odd one, because although it is classed as a non-durable timber, it is much loved by those seeking a light, good quality plywood for building small, light hulls; for instance, it has been very successfully used for canoe and dinghy building. And it is because of this light weight that it has a special dispensation under BS 1088 and can be classed as a marine plywood. It is best used in areas which are not in continuous contact with water. However, hulls built of gaboon plywood that are kept ashore and under cover are usually long-lived, and durability can also be much improved if they are protected by an epoxy coating. Light brown in colour, gaboon is a moderately priced board of great importance to the builders of small boats.

Meranti

Medium density with a medium to dark red colour, Meranti is durable and converts into a plywood which is ideal for hull construction, bulkheads and panelling that may come in contact with water. It is of moderate cost.

Mahogany

As a timber, mahogany is becoming increasingly controversial. However, steps are being taken to ensure that it is obtained from legitimate sources, and plywood is a very economical use of this valuable timber. The colour and grain texture depend on the country of origin, but in general it has a high strength, good resistance to fungal attack and is ideal in areas where the surface is permanently subjected to a cycle of wetting and drying. Proper mahogany plywood invariably has very high quality surface veneers. Some brand names carry Lloyds certification.

Teak-faced

This is less expensive than solid teak plywood; it is also significantly lighter. It is available with either one or two teak faces in a high grade of timber, and usually with ¹⁄₁₆in (1.5mm) surface veneer backed up by a BS 1088 marine plywood core. It is not really economical for building hulls, although its cost can be justified in exposed areas. It is relatively expensive.

Teak Decking

This is an economical form of simulated teak decking comprising a BS 1088 marine plywood inlaid with black or white strips to give the appearance of real caulked seams. It is usually restricted in use to larger vessels, but it can be employed very effectively for the decking or sole of a small boat. It is extremely expensive, but it can produce a striking result.

ADHESIVES

In recent years, modern technology has influenced virtually every sphere of life, and boat building is no exception. The one development that has had the greatest effect is undoubtedly that of modern adhesives. Arguably they have touched every aspect of wooden boat building, right through to the most traditional aspects of the craft. Of course, wooden boats are still being built without a lick of glue in them, but it would be a very pedantic builder who would throw away an otherwise perfect piece of timber because of a knot that could easily be repaired with a dab of epoxy and a small plug.

Modern adhesives have created a whole new spectrum of both materials and techniques, and these have completely revolutionized the design and building of small wooden boats – and to a large extent were responsible for keeping the craft alive during a period when modern plastics seemed to be replacing many of our natural building materials. We have already discussed the range of plywoods that now form the basis of a whole new branch of boat building, and without waterproof/ water-resistant glues they would never have been developed. But just as exciting has been the development of adhesives with sufficient strength and durability to completely replace traditional fastenings. Perhaps the best known is epoxy, a resin based on diglycidol ether of bisephenyl A. But there are a number of others which are just as valuable to today's builder of wooden boats, such as resorcinol- and poly-urethane-based adhesives. All have their more suitable applications and also their limitations, and these should be properly appreciated before use.

Some modern adhesives are not suitable for boat building, although at a glance their labelling might suggest otherwise. One example is PVA, or polyvinyl acetate glue. There are versions that are specified as water-resistant, but these fall far short of what is needed for boat building. Nevertheless, there is a significantly more important reason for mentioning this type of adhesive: it does not perform well under sustained loads. So although it might at first sight seem to be a cheap option for gluing together a building jig, for instance, strain on the jig exerted by bending the keelson, keel and stringers during hull construction could have undesirable effects.

Another one to avoid, although it is neither marketed nor sold as a timber adhesive, is polyester resin. This is a resin intended for making glass-reinforced plastics; it also has a limited application as a base resin for a filling compound such as is used for car-body repair. But it was never intended as a wood adhesive and should not be used as such.

The following gives a breakdown of adhesives which are suitable for boat building:

Epoxy Resin

Epoxy has been developed far beyond the status of mere glue, and has even been used in place of stringers. But it is as an adhesive that we are examining its properties, and a most impressive one it is!

Since it first became available, a whole range of brands has been launched onto the market, all claiming their own special advantages, although most popular brands offer similar characteristics. In general, it comes in two liquids, the resin and the hardener, which are mixed in varying ratios. It is important to be accurate when measuring out the quantities of resin and hardener, and that is especially so when preparing small amounts; a difference of just 1cc one way or the other can make a significant effect on the outcome. But measuring syringes and pumps make mixing epoxy very straightforward.

By itself, epoxy resin is relatively fluid and although it could be used as a wood adhesive, would present various problems not least of which would be the draining away from the adjoining surfaces. To improve its suitability as a wood glue, various formulations have been developed to thicken and give body to the basic resin, but many boatbuilders now favour the brands that offer a range of admixtures so that you can 'design' the adhesive to suit a particular job exactly. For instance, a glue texture suitable for easy application to a horizontal surface may well run off a vertical area, which would be better served by a thicker mix. The materials available for mixing

with the resin range from fine wood powder to colodia silia. Each bestows its own particular property and it is important to follow the brand maker's recommendations carefully. Also, epoxy fillers have to be handled with the utmost respect because they are by nature very fine, and if breathed in could cause problems.

Epoxy glues have many advantages over other adhesives, the two most important of which are that they are gap-filling and do not need high clamping pressures to create a perfect bond. However, this should not be used as an excuse for sloppy work. A further advantage of epoxy is that it produces a very unobtrusive glue line, which can be important in boat building where so much of the detailed work comes under close scrutiny. Things such as tillers and knees can, with a little care, be made to appear as if made from solid timber rather than having been laminated out of thin strips of timber.

Epoxy is not without its problems, and has to be used with care. Keep it off your skin, don't breath any fumes and don't leave large quantities in the pot to harden. Epoxy cures by creating its own heat, and a large mass can create sufficient heat to cause it to self-ignite. The other point about not mixing big batches at a time is that it is relatively expensive, and if you consistently mix 20cc when you only need 10cc for the job, the completed boat will cost far more then you bargained for; so be sparing.

Polyurethane Glue

Compared with epoxy, this is a relatively new adhesive which seems to be gaining great favour amongst the builders of wooden boats. It comes in an air-tight plastic container and is a darkish brown, single liquid that does not require mixing. The only drawbacks are that it has a limited shelf-life; it thickens when cold, and can become difficult to spread in its thickened condition; and if you get any on your hands, it will stay for a week before wearing off. It is not a gap-filling glue in the same way as epoxy, but it will fill gaps within a joint. The gluing surfaces need to be clamped tightly together to allow the polyurethane to make a firm bond. Any surplus that squeezes out, foams after a short contact with the air, and is relatively easy to clear away. So far, the two main applications seem to be for laminating frames, tillers and so on, and for gluing cedar strips together when building strip-planked hulls. It cures with a relatively unobtrusive glue line, does not dull the cutting tools, and forms a very strong bond. A further advantage is that, to date, we have not heard of any cases where users have become sensitive to the product.

Resorcinol Formaldehyde

This is another two-part adhesive which comes as a dark brown resin to which is added a hardener. It is classed as a water- and boil-proof glue. The two main brands are Aerodux (Ciba-Geigy) and Cascophen (Borden Chemicals). There is, in fact, very little difference between the two except that the hardener for Aerodux comes in a liquid form, whilst that for Cascophen is a powder. The shortcomings of resorcinol-based glues include an intolerance to low temperatures when curing, coupled with the relatively long setting time; a dark glue line which can detract from the aesthetics of the piece; and a need for pin-point accuracy when mixing the hardener with the resin. Their main benefit is extreme

durability which enables them to withstand long periods of weathering and also submersion in water without protection. They also make an extremely strong joint, and have a moderate gap-filling ability when thickened by adding a proprietary filler agent.

Urea Formaldehyde

Mainly due to the introduction of more durable, modern WBP glues such as epoxy, urea formaldehyde-based adhesives, of which Cascamite (Borden Chemicals) and Aerolite (Ciba-Geigy) are probably the two best known brands, are often overlooked by today's boatbuilders. The main reason is that they only have a moisture-resistant rating – they are not resistant to boiling water and their working life is limited to ten years. Their great advantages are cheapness, economy and easy application. Taking each point in turn: a urea-formaldehyde glue is a fraction of the cost of more advanced glues. It comes as a powder to be mixed with water: once mixed, it has a pot-life of about an hour in normal working temperatures – though less on a hot summer's day – and if small quantities are mixed at a time, waste can be kept to a minimum. It can be mixed either by weight, or by volume which is more convenient when dealing with small batches. It spreads easily and can be washed off hands and the workplace with water. Its durability is greatly enhanced when it is protected by a good paint system.

The real question to ask is whether or not it is appropriate for the job in hand. If you are using best quality plywoods and timber, then perhaps a strong case can be made for using the longest-lasting glues. But if, on the other hand, you are building a knockabout boat from cheaper, exterior grade plywood and less durable timber, you may well be satisfied with the prospect that your boat may only survive for about ten years. In which case there is little point in spending more money than is necessary on a glue that will outlast the useful life of the boat.

FASTENINGS

Boats have been described variously as 'including hundreds of pieces of wood held together with thousands of pieces of copper'. As far as traditional boats are concerned, little has changed, the only significant development in recent times being the introduction of bronze ring nails. These have a grip comparable with that of a screw, but they take a fraction of the time to drive, and are generally far more economical than their threaded counterparts.

Traditional Copper Boat Nails

Unlike normal 'household' nails which are round in section, boat nails are square with somewhat rounded points and round, slightly countersunk heads. The length is either specified in inches or millimetres, but the thickness is always given in standard wire gauge (SWG), the higher the number, the smaller the size; it is also useful to memorize that 16 gauge is $\frac{1}{16}$in (1.5mm), whilst 10 gauge is $\frac{1}{8}$in (3mm).

Boat nails can either be used for straight nailing, for securing the planks to the stem and transom, or in conjunction with little dished washers called roves – in which case the nail becomes a rivet.

In straightforward use, boat nails should never be driven into timber blind

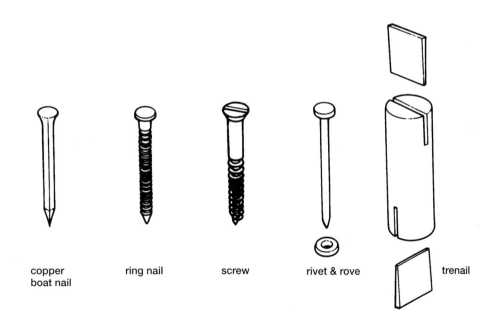

copper boat nail   ring nail   screw   rivet & rove   trenail

Selection of different fastenings.

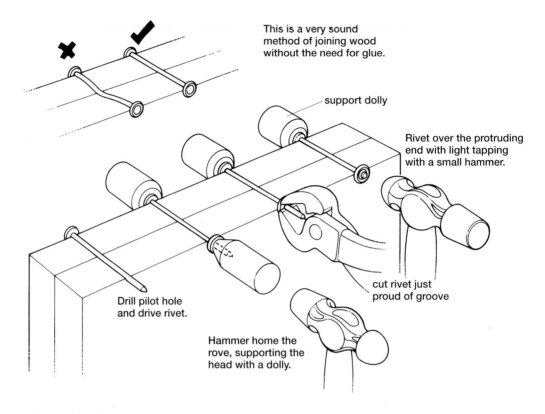

This is a very sound
method of joining wood
without the need for glue.

support dolly

Rivet over the protruding
end with light tapping
with a small hammer.

cut rivet just
proud of groove

Drill pilot hole
and drive rivet.

Hammer home the
rove, supporting the
head with a dolly.

Copper rivet and roving.

but pilot holes should be drilled: this will avoid the risk of bending the relatively soft nails whilst hammering them home. The pilot hole should be just a shade smaller than the measurement across the flats of the nail riveting – used extensively in traditional clinker construction for joining the overlapping planks – and securing timbers into both clinker and carvel hulls is relatively straightforward, but it is best done by two people, one working on the outside of the hull supporting the head of the rivet with a dolly, the other driving home the rove and clenching over the rivet on the inside of the hull. The procedure is shown very clearly in the diagram above.

The most critical stage of the task is driving the rove firmly home with a hollow punch against an accurately held dolly. Although it might be assumed that the dolly holder has the easier task, this is not so: it requires both strength to support the weight, combined with a sensitive touch to feel whether or not the head of the rivet is being properly supported. Failure to get this part right leads to problems during the following stage, which can cause the rivet to bend. Once the rove is securely home – it should hold itself firmly in place – the excess length of rivet can be trimmed off, leaving just sufficient to allow its end to be peened (riveted) over with numerous light blows using a ball-peen hammer (one with a rounded end), all the time supporting the head of the rivet with the dolly. Don't try to speed up the process by using a bigger hammer or heavier blows, because this will simply bend the rivet.

An alternative method of fastening a boat nail – without using a rove – is to drive it through the planks, turn the protruding end over a spike and then drive it back into the wood, hammering against the dolly supporting the head of the nail. Because it avoids the cost of a rove, this method of fastening is often regarded as inferior to a rivet and rove. But just as with peening over the rivet to finally secure the rove, light hammering is essential: heavy-handedness can crack the nail, which will subsequently fail under load.

Ring Nails

As we have already mentioned, ring nails have a far better grip than ordinary boat nails, provided they are used for the right applications – because it can also argued that the biggest drawback to a ring nail is the difficulty of extracting it. When used in modern construction techniques where the joint being nailed is also bonded with a permanent glue such as epoxy, being able to remove the nail so that, for instance, a section of planking can be replaced, is somewhat academic because the seam is not going to give up lightly anyway. But when traditional building methods are being employed, a strong argument in favour of traditional boat nails can be made.

The most usual choice, however, is not between the ring nail or boat nail, but between the ring nail and screw. As a general rule, if a ring nail will do the job, use it and avoid the extra cost, time and effort involved in using a non-ferrous screw.

Even so, ring nails should not be driven without first preparing the way with a small pilot hole; for much of the time you may get away without piloting, but inevitably some will bend and, when they do, they can make a terrible mess.

The only occasions where ring nails are inferior to screws is when a strong clamping action is needed to bring two surfaces together before the glue has cured, or when you want to hold parts together temporarily, when a combination of wood screws and ring nails may be appropriate.

Wood Screws

Like boat nails, wood screws are specified by length and standard wire gauge size. However, the point at which the diameter of the screw is measured is such that the shank – the unthreaded section just below the head – is greater than the SWG measurement. For instance, the shank of a No. 10 screw is $\frac{3}{16}$in (5mm) not $\frac{1}{8}$in (3mm) as the gauge size may suggest.

The shelves of the average DIY store will contain a confusing array of options as to the metal from which wood screws are made, to a whole range of head patterns, and even some with double-helix threads, sometimes referred to as 'quick-action screws'. For boat building, however, choose the standard countersunk headed wood screw in either brass or bronze, depending on the usage of the craft. Brass is perfectly satisfactory on small boats that are not kept in salt water, but a boat with brass screws left on a permanent mooring, and especially in salt water, runs the risk of electrolytic corrosion in its fastenings caused through a loss of zinc from the brass. Bronze, on the other hand, is both stronger and far less prone to this sort of corrosion.

Whichever you choose, time-consuming breakages can be avoided by first pilot drilling before driving in the screw; and when screwing into a hardwood, cut the thread in the timber by first driving home a steel screw. This may seem laborious, but it can save an enormous amount of effort should you be unlucky enough to break a screw off in its hole.

At face value, stainless steel screws should be the answer to a boatbuilder's dream; in reality, however, they are not. Above the waterline they can be used with confidence; the problem comes – or may come – when they are used below the waterline where, if you are unlucky, they can corrode at an alarming rate. There are actually two problems: that of identifying whether the stainless steel is, in fact, a marine grade (as used for propshafts, for instance) or just a general purpose grade; and whether the screw will suffer from shield or crevice corrosion, caused by the surface being either covered or scratched.

Trenails

The trenail or trunnel, derived from 'tree nail', is one of the oldest forms of boat fastening, and you might reasonably ask what relevance it has for today's boatbuilder. However, there are occasions when a screw or a boat nail can't be used, but a trenail will do nicely. One such application is where a screw has broken, and removing the stump has created a small crater. This can be drilled out and a trenail inserted, and the job will both look good and perform well. Trenails can also be used in a traditional manner when building in glued lapstrake (clinker), where the strakes can be temporarily held in place using nut-and-bolt clamps: the holes that result can be trenailed, which not only stops up the

holes but also strengthens the seams, provided the right size of trenail is used.

In its traditional form, a trenail is a hardwood dowel held in place by a pair of wedges driven from either end, the wedges positioned across the grain to avoid longitudinal splitting. To control the action of the wedges, small saw-cuts are made in the ends of the dowel to 'lead' the wedges into place. If the trenail is used blind (into a hole that doesn't pass all the way through the timber), the wedge is inserted into the slot before it is driven into the hole. The action of the wedge against the bottom of the hole drives it up into the trenail when it is tapped into place, so locking it in position. The outer wedge can then be driven home to complete the trenail fastening.

A more modern version can be made, using an adhesive in place of the wedges. If the trenail is being driven into a blind hole, it must be grooved along its length to allow excess glue to escape, so it can be driven all the way home.

PLASTICS

For most people, plastic immediately brings to mind glass-reinforced plastics, or GRP for short. Although the amateur builder can work in this medium, it is usually left to the professional builder using production-line techniques. Nevertheless, it is useful for the amateur to at least know the basics, if only to decide whether or not it is a sensible option for the type of boat he or she is considering building. The problem is that to produce a good result needs either a very expensive mould, or a high degree of skill in handling the material which is not, in itself, without problems of both health and safety.

To explain briefly, GRP is a combination of glass-fibre matting embedded in polyester resin – although other types of resin are sometimes used. The glass mat comes in three basic forms: chopped strand mat (otherwise known as CSM), woven rovings and combination mats. CSM is a type of glass felt, made up of randomly laid filaments. It is manufactured in various weights, starting from $\frac{1}{2}$oz/ft^2; for small hulls, $1\frac{1}{2}$oz/ft^2 is the usual choice. Woven roving is a coarse woven glass cloth which used to be specified in ounces per square yard (oz/yd^2) but is now almost universally specified in kg/m^2. The weave can be either bi-directional, which gives equal strength in two directions; or uni-directional, in which case the weave is biased in one direction, giving greater strength in that direction. Combination mats, as the name suggests, combine both CSM and roving, and are often very sophisticated in their make-up; they are designed specifically to confirm to compound curves, and do so more readily than either CSM or woven rovings. They also use far less resin which results in a much stronger laminate.

There are two basic types of resin, and two different formulations. The two typed are orthophthalic and isophthalic resins, and they are available as either a gel-coat resin or a laminating resin. The former is less expensive, but it does not resist water penetration as well as the latter, and for a long while, many boatbuilders have used a combination of isophthalic gel coat (the resin-rich surface layer) with orthophthalic laminating resin in an attempt to provide the added protection of the more expensive resin with the relative economy of the cheaper orthophthalic resin.

Production GRP hulls are usually produced in a female mould which is both expensive and time-consuming to produce. An alternative is sandwich construction: the core of the sandwich comes in the form of a purpose-made foam, which is fixed over a timber mould made in the form of the hull. GRP is then laminated over the foam, and when it has cured, the whole is removed from the frame and an inner lamination of GRP is placed inside the structure; this completes the sandwich.

Although it is possible to build small boats by this method, it is somewhat specialized and therefore beyond the scope of this book which concentrates on modern methods of wooden hull construction.

4 Boat-building Techniques

If this were a history of boat building, it would be in order to start looking at traditional building methods and techniques, moving on in a chronological manner until eventually we came to modern cold-moulding techniques using epoxy resins and even incorporating woven glass cloth. But the purpose of this book is to be of practical help to the reader, so we shall start at a time when contemporary boat-builders developed a whole new way of building small boats with plywood and glue, a way that has become known as the stitch-and-glue method. First, however, we will consider ways of joining two or more panels of plywood together to produce a continuous sheet.

There are two basic methods of achieving the same ends: **butt jointing**, which may seem by far the easier method, but has the disadvantage of being rather conspicuous and can also create 'hard' spots in the panel; and **scarfing**, which can look so neat as to be almost invisible, but which is more involved, demands a higher degree of basic skill, and has to be executed accurately. However, the task of scarfing is not half as difficult as some would have you believe. Scarf joints can also be used to join lengths of solid timber, so it is a particularly useful technique to master and one that allows a more economical use of materials.

BUTT JOINTS

These are sometimes known as 'strap joints' by virtue of the piece of wood that straps the two panels together. This type of joint is prepared by first ensuring that the

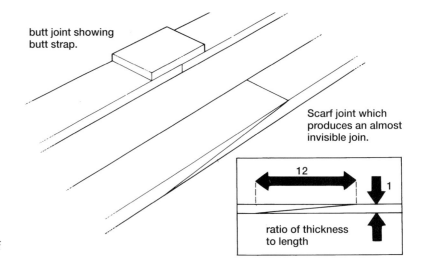

butt joint showing butt strap.

Scarf joint which produces an almost invisible join.

12

1

ratio of thickness to length

The two options for jointing planks or sheets of plywood end-to-end.

72

two edges to be joined are straight and square. The strap bridging the joint should be cut from the same type and thickness as the sheets being joined, with a width of around twelve to fourteen times the thickness of the plywood sheets. Ideally the strap's surface veneer grain should be aligned with that of the butt-jointed sheets; the result certainly looks better, and if the panel is to be bent round a tight curve, there is less likelihood of 'hard' spots in thinner panels. But if it comes down to the economical use of available materials, then sense should prevail.

Perhaps the most important point to remember when making a butt joint is that the two abutting edges should be well glued together. Failure to do this might lead to a weakened joint, and it could also allow water to penetrate the end grains within the panels, which can lay the seeds of rot.

There are several techniques of assembling the joint, the most important factor regarding all of them being to ensure that the panels line up accurately across the joint. Depending on the thickness, the joint can be fastened in a variety of ways, ranging from ring nails to simple wood screws. Thin panels, however, are best fastened using clenched copper boat nails. Using epoxy as an adhesive, it is possible to make a butt joint without any fastening at all, but the problem does arise of having to hold the panels and butt strap securely whilst the epoxy is hardening. One solution is to tack the panels and strap temporarily to a polythene-covered baseboard – but don't then forget to fill the holes from the temporary fastening.

SCARF JOINTS

This type of joint is used for both joining sheets of plywood and joining lengths of timber. The principles are basically the same, but the techniques vary, mainly to take account of the different thicknesses involved.

When scarfing plywood, the joint is formed by making two matching bevels along the full length of the edges to be joined. These bevels are brought down to a feather edge so that when the panels are brought together, there is no sign of a step

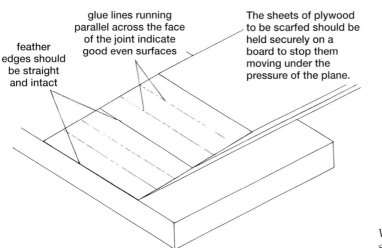

feather edges should be straight and intact

glue lines running parallel across the face of the joint indicate good even surfaces

The sheets of plywood to be scarfed should be held securely on a board to stop them moving under the pressure of the plane.

What it takes to make a successful scarf in plywood.

and the surface is virtually continuous. The advantage over the butt joint is that not only is it more aesthetic, but also the two panels, so jointed, will bend as one and as a result there is little loss of strength across the scarf.

The important factor is to cut both bevels at exactly the same angle – and thanks to the make-up of plywood, this is nothing like as difficult as it would seem, the trick being to plane both bevels at once. First you mark with a pencil the width of the bevel on each panel: usually a width-to-thickness ratio of 8:1 is used – it is possible to make a joint a little shorter, though note that in plywood there is no real advantage in making it significantly longer, because it only makes it more difficult to maintain a straight feather edge.

Having marked the two bevels, one on the face, the other on the back, the panels are brought together face-to-face, with the marked edges staggered and clamped down onto a straight, heavy board for planing. The method you use to clamp the panels to the support board depends on the situation, and it is sometimes a case of improvisation, but the generally accepted method is to use a heavy clamping batten with a slight convex curve worked into the clamping surface. G-clamps are used to cramp the ends of the batten down onto the support board, and the curve in the clamping batten provides even clamping across the full length of the scarf. Two points are worth remembering: leave sufficient space between the clamping batten and the area to be bevelled to handle the plane; and place the G-clamps screw downwards, so that when you lean over the work to sight the bevels, you don't take your eye out on the wing-screw.

An alternative method is to hold the panels down on the support board with tacks driven below the surface. The only problem with this is the high probability of catching a tack head with your beautifully shaped plane iron. It can also leave nail holes showing in the finished joint.

Having checked the positioning of the overlap, and that the panels are perfectly aligned, the most satisfying part of the job – planing the bevels – can begin. Taking your best hand plane with a finely set iron, and holding it at 45° to the direction of the edge, start planing the bevels, two or three

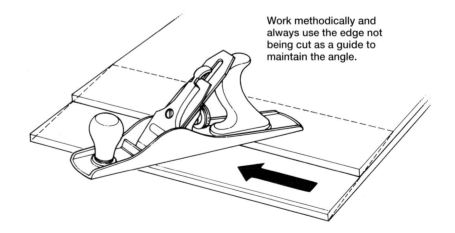

Work methodically and always use the edge not being cut as a guide to maintain the angle.

Making the first cut.

full-length passes in turn, supporting the plane sole on the panel not being cut on that pass. The width of the bevel increases with each pass of the plane, and soon it will be deep enough to reveal the glue line between the first and second veneers. As work progresses, a very satisfying pattern will develop, and it is this pattern of glue lines which will show whether the cut has been even across the full width of the panels. Curved lines indicate dips in the cut, and it is surprisingly easy to identify where the dips and valleys are and plane accordingly.

As the forward edge thins almost to the point of completion, it is important to keep a keen eye on your pencil marks which must not be planed out: once the line is lost you have nothing to work to, and accuracy is soon lost. When jointing relatively thin plywood, planing with a hand plane is the only sensible option. But when making scarfs in plywood of around ⅚in (8mm) and above, time can be saved by using an electronically powered hand planer – though only if you are experienced in the use of such a tool. Electric planers are particularly unforgiving and if not treated

with the greatest respect, can do untold damage to both plywood and flesh.

As work progresses, check that the bevels being created are flat by angling the plane to use the corner of the sole as a straight-edge. If a curve has developed, correct it with careful use of the plane; don't use a sandpaper block to do this, because it can make the situation worse. If it continues to be difficult you can correct the problem by accurately placing a batten so that it supports the rear of the plane's sole as a transverse cut is made.

Once the bevels are ready for gluing, turn the top panel over and mate up the tapering edges, and check that all is well before applying any glue. It is also useful at this point to mark a pair of datum lines so that you can check after gluing and clamping that the wedge-shaped joint surfaces have not been caused to slide under clamping pressure.

When you are happy that all is well, take the joint apart and apply glue in accordance with the manufacturer's instructions. Do not be over-generous! Provided you have not been over-enthusiastic at the planing stage, there should be no gaps to

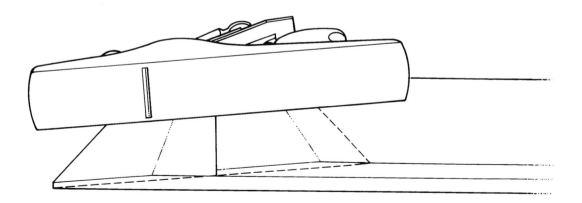

Checking with the edge of a plane for flatness – work progressively on each face.

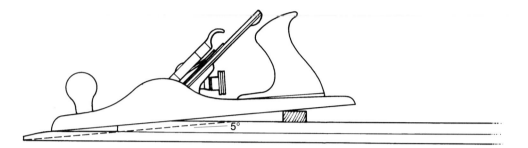

Resting the tail of the plane on a batten provides a guide to true up any curvature that may have developed.

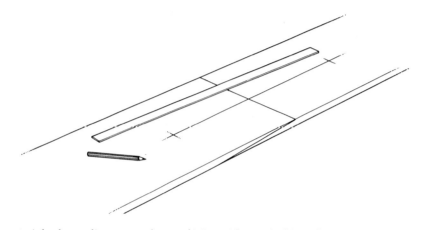

Drawing a straight datum line across the scarf joint with two 'tick' marks makes it easier to check that the joint has not slipped during gluing and clamping.

fill, so using a lot of glue only increases the problem of removing it once the clamps have been taken away.

One method of preventing the panels sliding under the pressure of the clamps is to tack the panels temporarily to the clamping board. The same clamping batten used when planing the bevels can be used to clamp up the glued joint, and covering the clamping board and batten with plastic sheet can prevent panel and clamps becoming one – though first check the compatibility of the plastic sheet with your chosen glue. It is surprising how some

glues will actually bond very efficiently to some plastics.

Scarfing Timber

The aim when cutting a scarf joint in solid timber is basically the same as when scarfing plywood, and with light sections of timber, it is possible to use the same technique of placing one piece on the other and planing both levels simultaneously. However, with larger sections of timber, or where, for practical purposes, the bevels cannot be planed together, it becomes necessary to cut them

Scarfing jig.

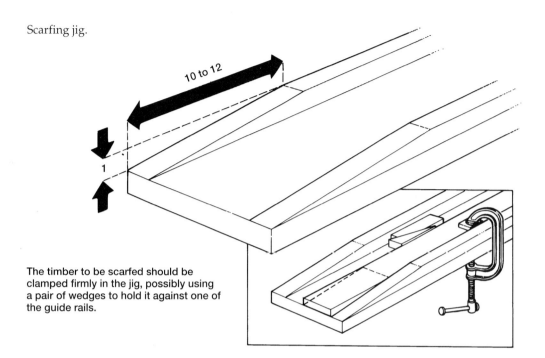

The timber to be scarfed should be clamped firmly in the jig, possibly using a pair of wedges to hold it against one of the guide rails.

separately. And if you have any number to cut – when strip-planking, for instance – it is worth taking the time to make a bevelling jig. This can take the form of a channel with sloping sides: the timber is clamped into the channel, and the sides of the jig form a guide for planing. The secret of success is careful marking out and working to the line. Never make a cut without being able to judge exactly how much material has been removed. It is also important to cut the bevels flat. Slight hollowness can be tolerated, but a convex surface results in an open glue line which is not only unsightly but may also be a potential weakness in the joint.

The length of the scarf depends largely on the application. Also, there are variations in the pattern of the scarf appropriate to different jobs.

When scarfing timber for masts, spars, oars, chine battens and so on where the joint relies totally on the glue, a relatively long scarf of 10:1 or better still, 12:1 should

be used, with the bevels ending in feather edges. When building up the keel section where heavier timber is involved, it is often beneficial to use a stopped scarf, sometimes known as a lipped scarf: as the name suggests, the bevel stops short of the feather edge. Again, the advantage is that there is less likelihood of the scarf picking up and splitting should the surface be run up against an obstruction. For this reason, the stopped scarf is commonly used for joining clinker and carvel planking. For certain applications such as rubbing strakes and covering boards, the lip is only put on the outside.

The ratio of length to thickness for these heavier scarf joints can be reduced to 6:1 where the joint relies only on fastenings, or 4:1 where the scarf is both screwed and glued. However, the rule is: the longer the better.

There are further variations of scarf joints, including hooked and stepped scarfs, but these are usually found in larger boats and are therefore outside the scope of this book.

STITCH-AND-GLUE

This is arguably the simplest form of boat building. It is, in fact, a modern version of a very old construction technique whereby planks were sewn together with leather thongs. One of the first boats to be built using the modern stitch-and-glue technique was the Mirror dinghy, of which thousands have been constructed. In comparison with the latest techniques, the method used on boats such as the Mirror could almost be described as crude; but it nevertheless worked well, and for those building their first boat it is a perfectly satisfactory method of construction. Having said that, as professional builders have seen the potential offered by the system, we have correspondingly seen a range of refinements

that answer all the criticism questioning the aesthetic appeal of stitch-and-glue. These will be covered in due course. Nevertheless, stitch-and-glue has remained largely, but not exclusively, an amateur method of building.

PREPARING THE PANELS

If you intend to develop your own small boat, you will by now be familiar with the panel shapes that, when joined together, create the basic hull shape. The first job when building full size is to scale up the panel sizes, very carefully marking them out on your 8ft-by-4ft sheets of plywood. It may be that the hull has panels which are longer than the 8ft (2.4m) provided by the standard sheet, in which case you must either find a plywood supplier who offers lengths over 8ft (2.4m), or joint the sheets to achieve the length needed.

Marking out is made more straightforward if the sheets of ply are scarf or butt

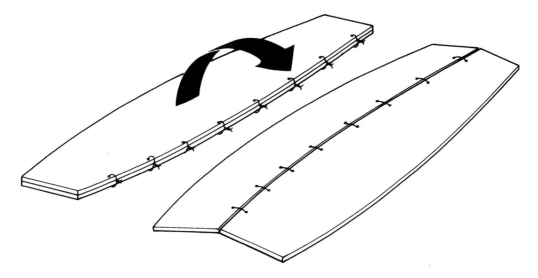

Stitching panels with wire. Insert stitches with panels flat and open to reveal their shape. Do not over-tighten stitches, as it could tear the plywood.

jointed beforehand. However, this will normally result is a 16ft (4.8m) length of ply which, even if you have the space, can be difficult to handle. If you are working to a professional design, this problem is usually sorted out. The designer will have prepared marking and cutting diagrams for each sheet of plywood that allows each component to be cut right to the line. Once cut, the individual are matched up and joined. Precise datum points are usually provided for setting up the length and straightness of each panel, and with very little effort you end up with a set of panels that, when stitched together, form exactly the shape intended.

If you are bold, it is possible to adopt the same strategy when working to you own design.

Alternatively the panels can be marked out roughly, leaving a generous margin all round, and can then be joined and marked out accurately. To do this, however, it is necessary to plan a datum line from which to mark the shape, approximately down the centre of the panel. This second method is well suited to home-grown designs, and although not so economical in the use of materials, it nevertheless provides the leeway that can avoid expensive mistakes.

Symmetry is vital. Even if you don't achieve exactly the panel shape you intended when working to your own design, this is by no means a disaster; the important thing is that two matching panels – two side panels, for instance – should be exactly the same size and shape. And don't forget that you need a left and a right

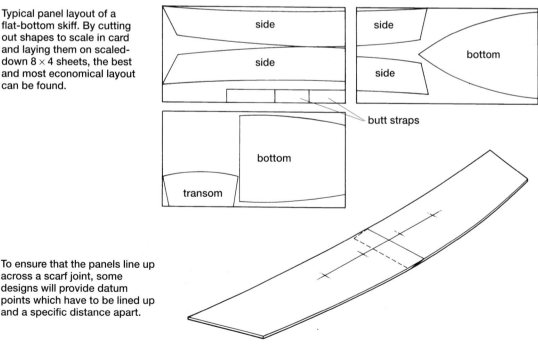

Typical panel layout of a flat-bottom skiff. By cutting out shapes to scale in card and laying them on scaled-down 8 × 4 sheets, the best and most economical layout can be found.

side
side
side
side
bottom
side
butt straps
bottom
transom
bottom

To ensure that the panels line up across a scarf joint, some designs will provide datum points which have to be lined up and a specific distance apart.

Arranging panels for economical cutting.

hand. There are times when this is of little consequence, but if the panels are butt jointed, two right-hand panels, although exactly the same shape, will result in the butt strap being on the outside of the boat on the port side. Even the roughest boat-builder will find this difficult to accept.

DRILLING THE HOLES

The stitches, either wire or nylon filament, that hold the panels together, prior to tap-ing, are made through pairs of holes drilled about ½in (13mm) in from the edges of the matching panels. However, it is not accu-rate enough simply to mark round each edge and space the holes at equal intervals; that approach works along the keel where a pair of bottom panels meets along a central seam, but all the others must be drilled to match. Start with the bottom panels or panel if your boat has a flat-bottomed hull.

If it is a Vee-bottomed boat, only one of the pair of panels need be marked. Draw the guideline ½in (13mm) in from the edges of the keel and chine. Then mark in the hole positions equally spaced about 6in (15.2cm) apart. Place the panels together, inside face to inside face, and clamp them firmly, mak-ing sure they are flat. Drill the holes, drilling both panels at once.

Now, lay the panels out flat, inside faces upwards, side by side. Then lay the adja-cent side panels alongside, making sure that they are aligned so that when bent round into shape, the ends of the seams will line up. At this stage, where the bottom panels lie right alongside the side panels, mark the first hole in the lower edge of each side panel. Then mark and drill two or three more holes on either side, simply spacing them the same distance as used in the bottom panels. The remaining holes are drilled as the stitches are being inserted: this way you ensure that the holes line up

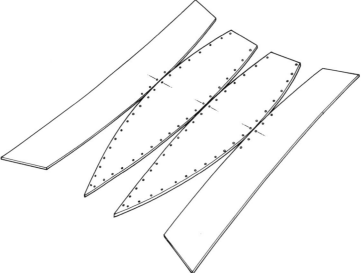

The two bottom panels on a Vee-bottomed hull can be placed face-to-face, and all the holes drilled. Side panels, however, should be drilled as assembly progresses.

On well-rounded hull sections com-bined with modest beam, it is possi-ble that all holes can be pre-drilled.

Sequence of drilling holes for wire stitches.

fairly accurately and don't detrimentally affect the lining up of the panels.

STITCHING

There are various methods of stitching the panel together, ranging from the basic copper wire staple that remains partially in place, to staples that are removed completely before taping. When stitch-and-glue was first developed, copper wire was used, and the insides of the stitches remained in place beneath the glass tape. The wire ends are usually twisted on the outside of the hull and snipped off before the inside of the seam is taped. This technique results in a lumpy appearance on the inside of the hull, although it has nevertheless worked well; and if speed is important or where the inside of the hull is not seen, as with a kayak for instance, it is still worth considering.

Some designers have advocated the use of nylon filament – around 50lb breaking strain –instead of wire, the panels being sewn together by a type of blanket stitch. The advantage over wire is that the outside of the joint can be taped first, over the filament, allowing the inside parts of the stitches to be removed prior to taping; thus the tape will lie completely flat along the inside, giving a much improved appearance. The only disadvantage is the limited tension that can be applied to the nylon filament; far more force can be applied to a twisted wire.

Another approach was to use plastic-covered wire. The theory is that the resin used to glue the tape in place will not bond to the plastic. Therefore once the joints have been taped on one side – usually the outside, with the wires twisted on the inside of

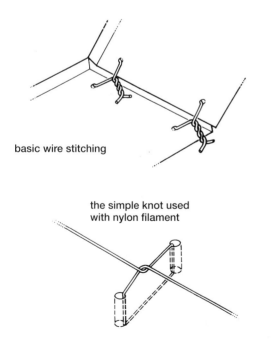

basic wire stitching

the simple knot used
with nylon filament

Wire or nylon filament?

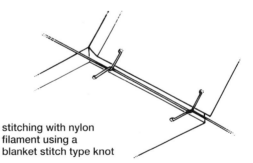

stitching with nylon
filament using a
blanket stitch type knot

On some hulls, a combination of nylon filament and copper wire twists gives the best results. The nylon is used where stresses are small; the wire is used where more pull is required.

the hull – the complete wire tie can be undone and withdrawn before the second side is taped. The disadvantage of this method is that the wire ties can't always be persuaded to pull through, or to come out leaving the plastic coating behind.

It is, of course, possible to use a combination of techniques, using copper wire where the panels need to be stressed together, and nylon filament where they pull easily into place or where it is difficult to get a wire tie into place.

The order in which the stitches are made depends somewhat on the design of the boat, but in general you should start by wiring the two bottom panels together along the keel joint. The most straightforward approach is to place the two bottom panels together, inside to inside, and loosely wire them with just a couple of twists to hold the ties in place. These panels can then be opened out to approximately the right deadrise angle, forming the curve of the keel ('deadrise' is the angle of the bottom panel from the horizontal). It may be necessary to put in a temporary frame at this point to hold the two bottom panels at the right angle. Once you are happy that all is well, the wire stitches can be tightened. It is important to close the seam without any overlap; the inside corners should come together, leaving a V-channel on the outside.

Once you are satisfied with the keel joint, the side panels can be added. Start in the middle, working outwards towards bow and stern. At this point you will also have to start drilling more holes opposite the ones predrilled when the panels were flat. This is one occasion when a power tool really is superior to muscle power, and the best is a rechargeable, cordless drill. It can be used one-handed and its relatively slow speed gives delicate control.

BOWS AND STERNS

If you are building a canoe or a canoe-stern boat, the bow and stern can be wired together in a similar fashion to the keel and chines. However, if the boat has a stern transom, or perhaps two transoms in the case of a pram, you will have to consider carefully how they are to be fitted. Those working to a proprietary design will simply follow the designer's instructions, but if you are exploring your own design it is helpful to have this point worked out well in advance.

There are three main options: a straightforward plywood transom subsequently framed with timber; a timber-framed transom fitted before taping the keel and chine seams; or a framed transom fitted after the longitudinal seams have been taped.

The simple solution is a plywood transom stitched and glued into the boat using a technique similar to that used to make the longitudinal seams along keel and chines. The weight and extent of the frame depends on the thickness of the plywood, and whether or not the transom is intended to carry an outboard engine. A bow transom of, say ⅜in (10mm) plywood would only need a light T-frame, whilst a stern transom of ¼in (6mm) plywood would need a well braced, all-round framing.

The procedure is to fit the plywood transom inside the bottom and side panels, creating the Vee-gap on the inside of the hull. When this is wired firmly into place, the Vee is filled with a loaded epoxy – an epoxy mix with a relatively high proportion of filler. (The details of this and the taping procedure are looked at later.)

If you have lofted the lines of the hull, you may be able to lift off the bevel angles between the bottom and the side panels,

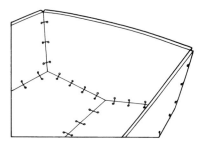

A simple plywood transom stitched and glassed into place.

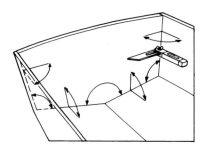

But before applying the glass and resin make sure the angles are correct.

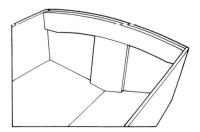

A simple Tee frame can be fitted once the plywood transom has been glassed in place.

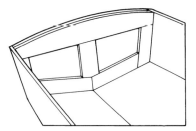

A fully framed transom which can be fitted at the same time as the longitudinal seams are glassed, or later on.

and the transom, in which case it is a practical proposition to make the fully framed transom on the bench. If you work accurately, it will be possible to glue and screw it in place before taping the keel and chine seams. The benefit of fitting the transom in this way is that it helps preserve symmetry. If the side bevels are angled exactly the same and the transom is presented square to the keel, you have a very good starting point from which to avoid a twisted hull.

The third option, of fitting the framed transom subsequent to taping the longitudinal seams, is done by setting up the hull with a temporary transom. This is replaced by the permanent transom after the taped seams have cured. The temporary transom, wired firmly into place, is used to give form to the hull in the initial stages, and

as a reference from which to measure the side and bottom bevel angles using an adjustable bevel gauge. The advantage of this approach is that it allows any slight variations to be evened out.

SETTING UP

Once the hull has been assembled, it takes on its own shape which, because of the flexible nature of relatively thin plywood, is not necessarily the final shape intended by the designer. A couple of braces which push out the gunwale to its full beam will possibly solve the problem; if not, it may be necessary to build one or two temporary frames from scrap pieces of timber and ply. Another trick to pull her into shape is to attach the

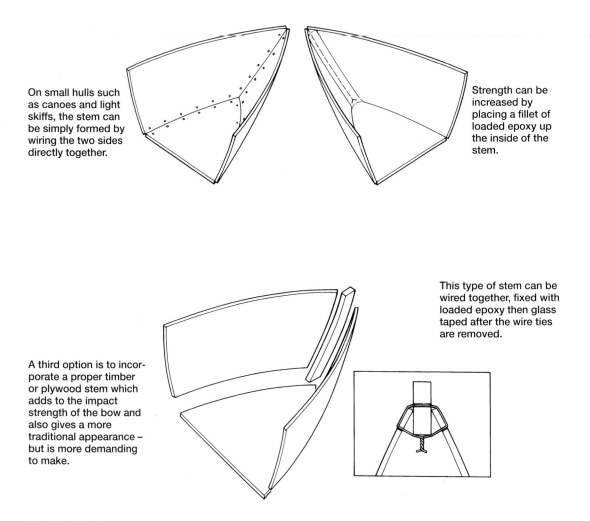

On small hulls such as canoes and light skiffs, the stem can be simply formed by wiring the two sides directly together.

Strength can be increased by placing a fillet of loaded epoxy up the inside of the stem.

This type of stem can be wired together, fixed with loaded epoxy then glass taped after the wire ties are removed.

A third option is to incorporate a proper timber or plywood stem which adds to the impact strength of the bow and also gives a more traditional appearance – but is more demanding to make.

Forming the stem.

gunwale stringers. Indeed, where the boat is relatively light and of modest beam, it is sometimes an advantage to fit one set of gunwale stringers before wiring the side panels into place. But don't be over-ambitious: a surprising degree of stress is created at the surfaces of a batten when it is bent, and a stout gunwale stringer glued onto a plywood panel in the flat can be extremely difficult to bend.

Rectifying Longitudinal Twist

With the hull generally persuaded into the desired shape, the next problem to check for and rectify is longitudinal twist. Before taping it can be rectified but it cannot be after, and a twist built into a stitch-and-glue hull is there for life. There are various methods for identifying twist, from sighting by eye to measuring, or dropping perpendicular lines down from taut line rigged between the centre line of the transom to the centre of the bow. What does it matter if a boat has a small amount of twist, you may ask. Well, when the boat is afloat, unless you meet someone with a very good eye, it will go totally unnoticed. Put the boat upside-down on a car roof-rack, however, and the problem will make itself only too apparent.

This course of action indeed provides the clue to the solution. Erect two horizontal bars about a third of the boat's length apart and a little wider than its beam. Place the wired-up hull, gunwale down, onto these bars, with the centre line of the hull at right-angles to them: any twist in the hull will manifest itself as a wobble. By lashing the hull down to the bars, the twist

is automatically eliminated. But having done so, one further check must be made. Set the angle of an adjustable bevel to the angle between the transom and the side of the boat on one side. Check the bevel against the transom-to-side angle on the opposite side of the hull: they should be exactly the same. If they are not, re-examine the symmetry of the hull and even check that each panel has been put in the right way round; on some multi-chine designs, it is possible to become confused.

Until you are absolutely happy with both symmetry and straightness, don't be tempted to move on to the next stage, which is gluing the whole structure together with glass tape and resin.

In the past, polyester resin has been used for this stage with a measure of success. Its

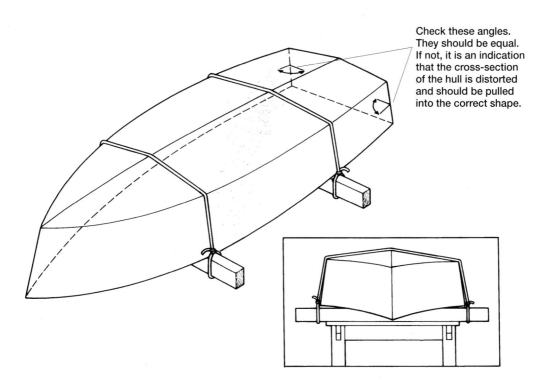

Check these angles. They should be equal. If not, it is an indication that the cross-section of the hull is distorted and should be pulled into the correct shape.

Putting a hull into shape over two parallel bars to eliminate twist before taping the seams.

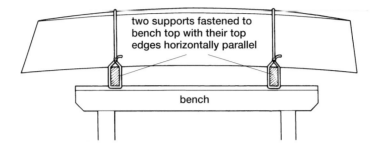

two supports fastened to
bench top with their top
edges horizontally parallel

bench

The illustration shows a simple hull form but the principle holds good for more complicated hull forms.

main disadvantage is, however, that it has a limited life. If well painted and protected from the weather, such a boat may last for ten years or more, but with rough treatment, it may not! The factors to balance out are the relative cost (polyester resin is far less expensive), against the potential usable life of your boat.

TAPING

If you intend to use the basic method whereby half the wire stitch is left in place, a more satisfactory result can be achieved by first going round the inside of each one with a light cross-pene hammer, gently tapping the wire into the corner of the seams. The inside tapes can then be applied.

The procedure is much the same whether you decide to use polyester or epoxy resin. To limit the spread of the resin and to help make a neat job, masking tape can be placed parallel to each seam and approximately 1¼in (30mm)) from the actual joint. This also provides a useful guide for placing the tape. Before you mix and spread the resin, lay the tape Along the seams, cutting it to length and then rolling it into neat rolls so that it can be

applied to the seam quickly and without fuss.

Mix a small quantity of resin following the manufacturer's instructions and spread it evenly along the seam, between the strips of masking tape. Only mix a small quantity at first. You will soon get to know how far a particular quantity will spread, and it is better to have to mix more, than to have expensive resin hardening in the pot. Also, don't apply the resin too thickly: it will only cause the glass tape to float away from the surface of the plywood, resulting in a weak joint. Now the glass tape (usually 2in/50mm wide) can be placed along the seam, working smoothly along the joint and again using the masking tape as a guide.

Once the glass tape is laid gently in place, it must be completely embedded into the resin. This is done by using a stippling action with a stiff resin brush – avoid using a brushing action because that will disturb the weave of the tape. When fully impregnated, the glass tape will all but disappear; white patches indicate inadequate impregnation, the remedy for which is more stippling or even a gentle roll with a roller. You may have to add a little more resin, but be sparing – too much, as we

Steps involved in making a
glass tape and resin joint.

Step 1 Ensure that all the
wire stitches are holding the
panels inside corner to inside
corner, and bend the inside
of the loop to bear against
the panels.

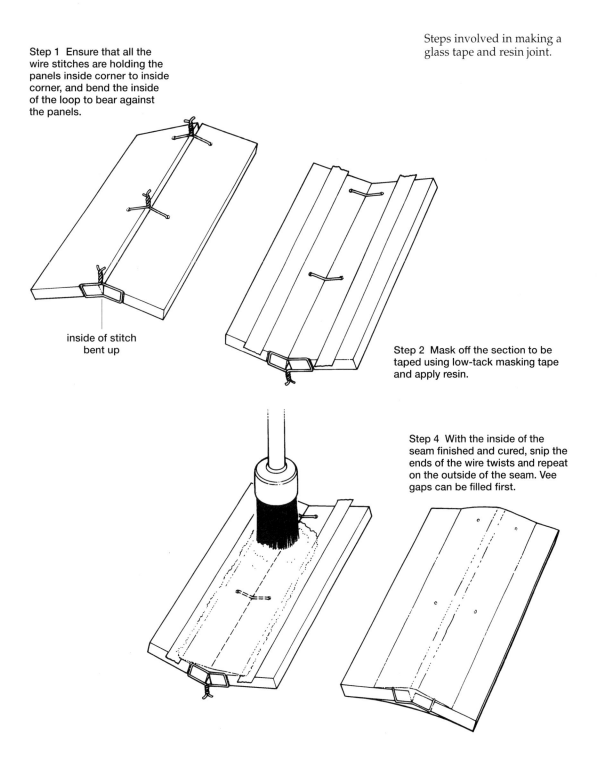

inside of stitch
bent up

Step 2 Mask off the section to be
taped using low-tack masking tape
and apply resin.

Step 4 With the inside of the
seam finished and cured, snip the
ends of the wire twists and repeat
on the outside of the seam. Vee
gaps can be filled first.

87

have said, is as bad as too little. Once you are satisfied with the result and before the resin hardens, carefully remove the masking tape and dispose of it where any resin that has collected will not get either on your boat or on the floor.

When the inside seam is properly cured, the wire stitches can be untwisted and, if plain wire, snipped off flush with the surface, or if plastic covered, pulled out. Once this task is complete, the outside can be taped, using a similar technique to that used on the inside.

A more sophisticated approach is to edge-glue the panels by filling the Vs using loaded epoxy. This provides a strong enough bond between the panels to allow the wire stitches to be removed completely prior to taping. With care, this method produces a seam that is virtually invisible.

The task of getting a perfectly smooth finish can also be made much easier if the epoxy is covered with a strip of polythene before it has cured; this can be gently rolled and then removed once it has cured. The final result, however, is gained by patient and gentle work using fine sandpaper (wet-and-dry) – but don't be over-enthusiastic and sand through into the glass tape.

FITTING OUT

We have now got a basic hull which, if care has been taken in the setting up, should be straight and true; but this in itself is a considerable achievement. The next stage is fitting out: installing frames, seats, rubbing strakes and so on. If you are working from a bought design, the details of all these should be clearly shown. However, for those who are working to their own designs, this is a very important stage because it influences the stiffness and, therefore, the ultimate strength of your craft.

We must visualize forces acting on the hull that will twist and distort its shape. Perhaps the most effective way of doing this is by first examining a model, holding it in your hands and gently applying twisting, bending and straightening forces. What you are looking for are changes in the angles where one panel meets another. For instance, apply slight inward pressure on the bow and stern and watch how the gunwale amidships moves outwards; this is mainly because the angle between the side and bottom panels is changing. Likewise, apply a torsional twist between the bow and stern and see how the angles between the gunwales and transom change.

By identifying all these areas where shape is affected by the stresses placed on the hull, it is possible to establish which places need additional bracing, and also to see the effects of adding structural members into the hull shell. Basically, the aim is to brace the hull in a way that will resist the forces which would otherwise cause distortion. Some methods are more effective that others, and one should always consider the weight implication. Supporting the seats, providing some form of buoyancy, and giving a measure of protection to the gunwale and the bottom of the boat are the first steps towards stiffening up an otherwise flexible hull.

Creating Buoyancy

There are several ways to prevent a small boat sinking should it become swamped. Apart from buoyancy bags, the most straightforward is to build sealed tanks into the bow and the stern; moreover the box structure so produced will add a great deal of rigidity to the ends of the boat. The

1. Applying a twisting force between stem and stern creates stress in corners of transom and stem.

2. Squeezing the gunwale amidships stresses all the seams and increases rake on stem and stern.

3. A load acting at the centre of the hull when it is afloat tends to push the gunwales outwards, which in turn forces the tops of the stem and transom inwards.

4. Adding thwarts, knees and a breasthook helps the hull resist all these forces.

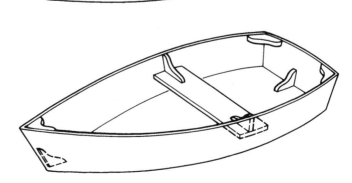

Forces acting on a hull to push it out of shape.

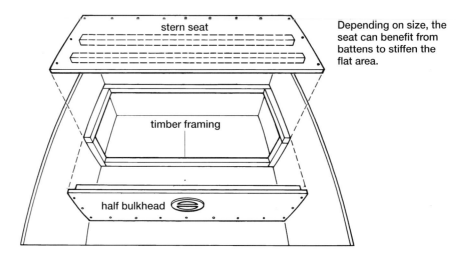

Depending on size, the seat can benefit from battens to stiffen the flat area.

Basic construction of a simple buoyancy tank/stern seat. An alternative to the timber framing for the half bulkhead is to bond it in position with epoxy fillets.

easiest way to do this is to build in two vertical bulkheads up to seat height, and then install braced plywood tops to form enclosed chambers. The bulkheads can be either glass taped in place, secured with epoxy fillets, or glued and screwed to timber battens. The tops can also be screwed and screwed down onto a light timber frame.

The way to mark out these panels of plywood is by a process called spiling, and one which we will return to time and again. It involves using a piece of scrap board as a template that fits loosely into the space where the panel is to be fitted. One edge should be used as a datum – when fitting a bulkhead, the top edge is usually the most convenient reference.

The next stage is to bridge the gap between the line along which the panel is to fit, and the edge of the template. This can be done in a number of ways: by using a pair of compasses to draw a series of arcs from the fitting line onto the scrap panel; by using a spiling block – a parallel-sided gauge – to mark a parallel datum line on the template in a similar fashion to that of using compasses; and by tacking short battens onto the template to create a series of fixed points around the template.

Of the three options, I much prefer the latter. If the same thickness of board is used for both template and panel, allowance for any bevels is automatically included, there is less likelihood of the template moving during the spiling process, and it leaves less scope for inaccuracies to creep in when marking out the panel.

It is never a good idea to seal off an area of the hull completely – nature is very effective at breaking such seals and water will get in, which not only defeats the object but also risks rot setting in. Far better to install small hatches, and there are some very effective bolt-in hatches made for the purpose.

Fitting the Centre Thwart

Boxing in the ends of the hull will have added an enormous amount of structural

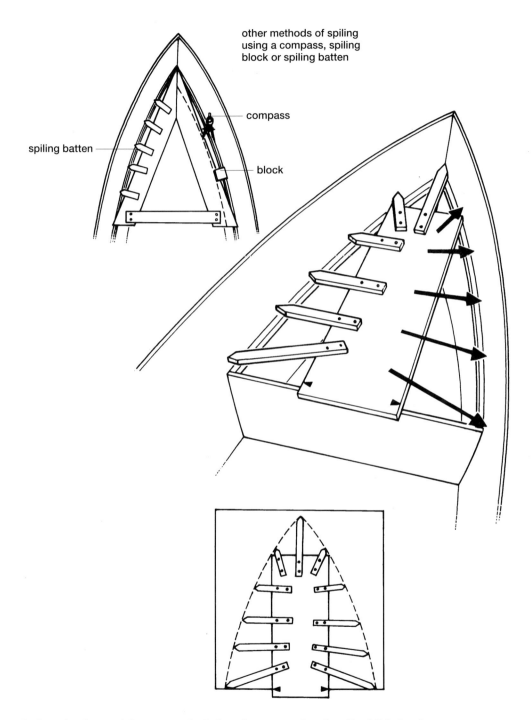

other methods of spiling
using a compass, spiling
block or spiling batten

compass

spiling batten

block

Spiling the shape of the top panel of a bow buoyancy chamber. Establish the shape on the hull and then transfer the shape onto the plywood panel – remember to take account of bevels.

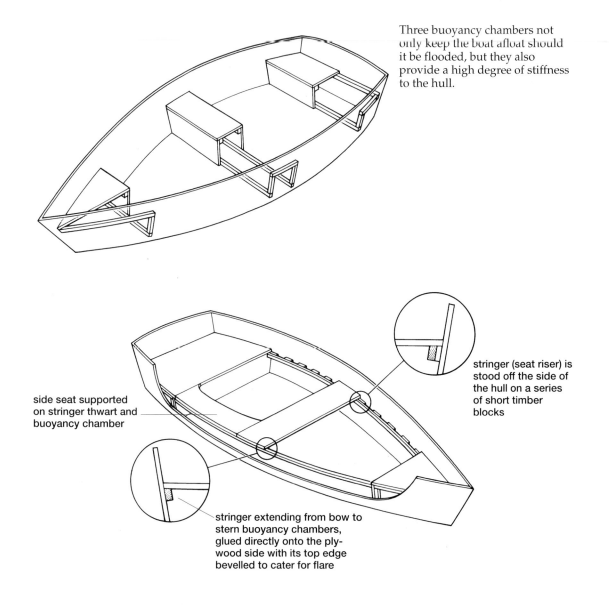

Three buoyancy chambers not only keep the boat afloat should it be flooded, but they also provide a high degree of stiffness to the hull.

stringer (seat riser) is stood off the side of the hull on a series of short timber blocks

side seat supported on stringer thwart and buoyancy chamber

stringer extending from bow to stern buoyancy chambers, glued directly onto the plywood side with its top edge bevelled to cater for flare

Thwart supports (two methods).

stiffness, but with the limited effect on the tendency for the hull to flex at the gunwale amidships. The most effective device here is the centre thwart. In its simplest form it can be a plank located at the sides by blocks of timber (cleats) that are slightly curved to sit neatly against the boat sides. Such a thwart, however, has one major disadvantage in that it does not spread the forces very far: should the side of the boat be run along the edge of the jetty or along a post, the hard spot formed by the end of the thwart may split the plywood.

Furthermore, a central thwart fitted on simple blocks does very little to reduce twisting in other areas of the hull. However, if it is fitted to stringers that extend well towards the bow and stern, and possibly support the fore and aft seats also, then we begin to see a far more effective structure coming into play. And if those stringers are stood off the sides of the hull either on short blocks or vertical frames, the overall structural stiffness is greatly increased.

Fitting Inwales

Next comes the fitting of inwales: these are battens running along the top inside edges of the hull, either screwed and glued directly onto the plywood, or stood off on short spacers positioned every 9in (23cm) or so. The advantage of the second option is that, for virtually the same weight of timber, it provides greater width and therefore far greater stiffness. However, on relatively thin plywood hulls, such inwales should only be used in conjunction with an external gunwale rubbing strake to provide continuous support to the outside of the gunwale.

Making Knees and Breasthooks

By now the hull will have stiffened up considerably, as compared to when it was a bare open shell. But there is one further addition necessary: the fitting of knees and a breasthook. Roughly speaking these are brackets, fitted across the corners to prevent the angles changing when under

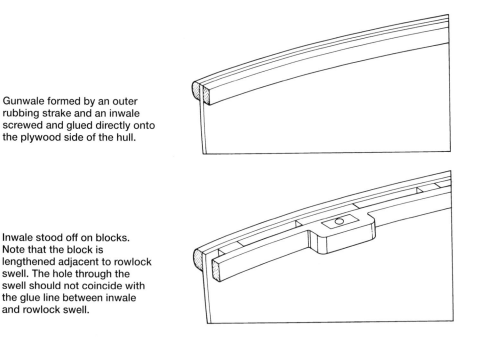

Gunwale formed by an outer rubbing strake and an inwale screwed and glued directly onto the plywood side of the hull.

Inwale stood off on blocks. Note that the block is lengthened adjacent to rowlock swell. The hole through the swell should not coincide with the glue line between inwale and rowlock swell.

Inwale construction.

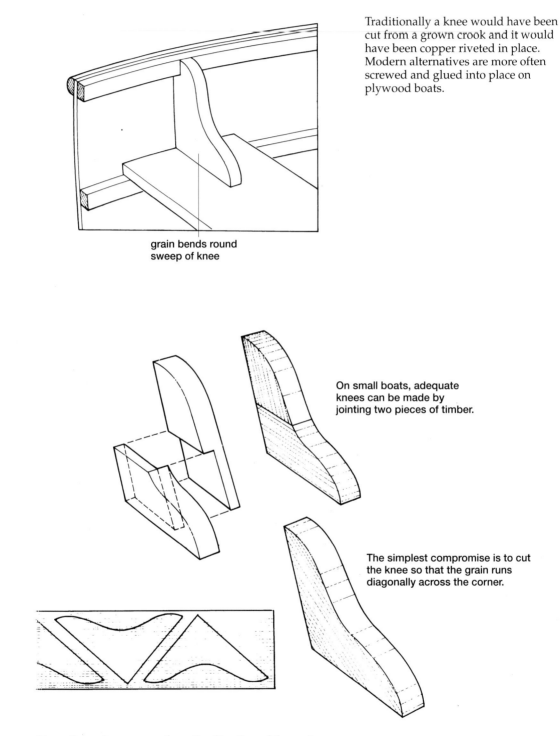

Traditionally a knee would have been cut from a grown crook and it would have been copper riveted in place. Modern alternatives are more often screwed and glued into place on plywood boats.

grain bends round sweep of knee

On small boats, adequate knees can be made by jointing two pieces of timber.

The simplest compromise is to cut the knee so that the grain runs diagonally across the corner.

Strength in a knee comes from the direction of the grain.

94

stress. There are two types of knee: **lodging knees** that are fitted horizontally, and **hanging knees** that are fitted vertically. **Breasthooks** are a specialized form of lodging knee, used to brace across the acute angle formed at the bow.

Traditionally boatbuilders would select timber, usually oak, that had a natural bend in the grain – for example where two branches forked – to fashion knees. Nowadays, however, only a few have the luxury of being able to search the forest for grown hooks. You may find a 'proper' timberyard willing to set aside some for you, but they are rare. With modern glues, however, there are alternative methods of making knees, almost as good as grown ones. And it is also possible on small boats to accept the second-best solution of simply using good, straight-grained timber with the grain running from mating face to mating face. Indeed, on boats with glued construction it can be argued that such knees are virtually as good, and a lot cheaper.

The other alternative is to laminate thin strips of timber to produce the required angle. Either the whole of the knee can be laminated, or just part, and quite often a mix of timbers can produce a very pleasing result. A simple jig can be made to form the shape of the laminate, and chipboard is a good material for the job. The jig takes the form of a base board onto which is screwed a curved former, and the strips of timber can be clamped round this whilst the glue is curing. A few strategically placed holes drilled into the former can ease the task of clamping, and polythene sheeting placed over the base board and round the curved surface of the former will prevent the knee blank and the former becoming one.

The curve on the former should be that of the inside of the knee, and this demands

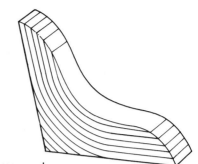

The corner can be made of a solid block.

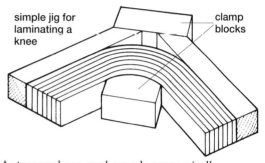

simple jig for laminating a knee

clamp blocks

A stronger knee can be made economically by laminating from thin strips of timber.

a little pre-planning to ensure that the angle between the mating faces can be worked in successfully.

Alternatively, the laminations can be clamped into a 'female' jig as shown in the above illustrations. Gluing up the laminates should be straightforward, but it can be made difficult if the strips of timber are not perfectly parallel in section. The only other possible problem is the laminates floating when the clamps are tightened. However, with a little patience and the odd panel pin, this can be easily overcome.

Because breasthooks usually span a relatively acute angle, it is often more practical to construct the blank using a sandwich technique. And if you decide to make a really fancy job, it is also possible to lay in

95

strips of contrasting timber. Usually a two-layer sandwich is sufficient, but by making one layer a little thicker than the other, the chances of screwing into the glue line are reduced.

Fitting Knees

There are two distinct stages involved in fitting a knee or breasthook, and unless the first stage is accurately done, the second is doomed to failure. Start by establishing the basic angle that the knee is to span: in some circumstances this can be done by using a sliding bevel gauge, simply setting the gauge against the angle at the widest point. However, there are times when a knee will have to joggle around a more complicated shape, in which case it is probably best to make a template out of thin plywood. But look carefully at the way in which the knee will eventually fit, and ensure that the template takes account of any bevels that may need to be cut in the knee for making the final fitting.

Once you have established the basic shape, then it is time to think about the bevels. The secret is not to try and judge any of them by eye – it must not be a case of trial and error because what is cut from one face, directly affects the fit of the other. Here the adjustable bevel gauge really proves its worth. Always set the gauge at right-angles to the face being fitted, and as each face is bevelled, make constant checks with the gauge; it is very easy to remove too much wood, but rather difficult to replace it. Also, don't assume that the two sides of the hull are absolutely equal. They should be, and this may be the time to make them so. But the angles and bevels should be established by measurement, not guesswork.

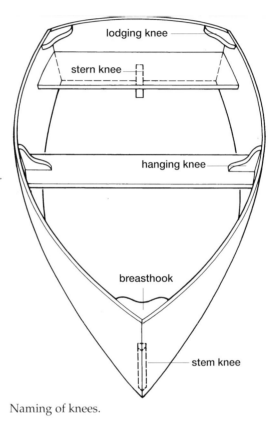

Naming of knees.

Traditionally, knees would be fastened in place by copper rivets passing right through the area they were reinforcing, and would not be glued in place. A hanging knee supporting the thwart in a clinker boat, for instance, would have rivets passing right through the knee to the underside of the thwart and to the outside of the planking. But the more rigid construction of a plywood boat allows the knee to be glued and screwed in place. Theoretically, one should be able to rely solely on the glue, especially if an epoxy glue is used. A stout fastening, however, can reinforce the joint across the grain, resulting in a stronger overall job.

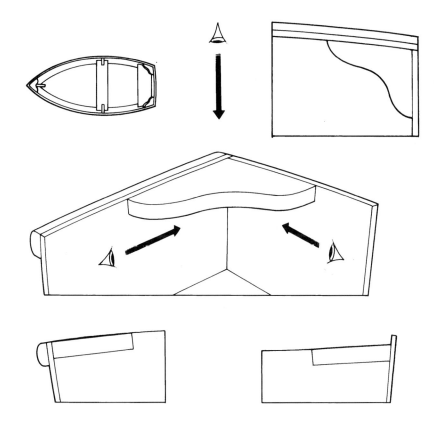

Looking into a corner between the transom and the side of a hull where a knee is to be fitted shows that every angle, on the two adjacent sides is different and needs to be measured accurately.

FINISHING OFF

With buoyancy tanks, thwarts, gunwale stringers and knees all installed, attention can be turned towards such things as rowlock swells, a skeg and perhaps a keel, rubbing strakes, making bottom boards and painting. All of these are quite straightforward, and if working to your own design you can copy details from similar-sized boats. The rowlock swells, however, should be positioned to place the rowlocks 9in (23cm) behind the after-edge of the thwart on which the oarsman will sit.

5 Sharpie Construction

Traditionally the sharpie had a flat bottom planked across the boat (athwartships) instead of having the more usual fore-and-aft planking found on dories and most British flat-bottomed boats. However, there is absolutely no reason why the same hull form should not be used in conjunction with plywood and modern glues to produce a perfectly sound flat-bottomed dinghy.

It is said that a traditional sharpie can be built in just eight stages including painting, and I can see no reason why the same should not also be true when building one in plywood.

STAGE ONE: MAKING A PAIR OF SIDES

If you follow true sharpie tradition you will have a plumb stem which, combined with a flare amidships, has rather a flattening effect on the degree of rocker in the forward section. In fact, it means that the bottom edges of the side panels can be made absolutely straight. However, if you wish to modify your sharpie to give her an angled stem, then the bottom edges of the side panels may have to be slightly curved to avoid too much rocker in the bow. And if you decide to follow the lines of the more developed modified sharpies, then the bottom edges of the side panels will be slightly 'S'-shaped, creating a pronounced rocker at the stern and an almost straight section towards the bow. The traditional sharpie

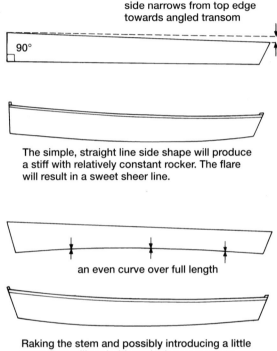

side narrows from top edge towards angled transom

90°

The simple, straight line side shape will produce a stiff with relatively constant rocker. The flare will result in a sweet sheer line.

an even curve over full length

Raking the stem and possibly introducing a little more flare will probably make it necessary to introduce a curve into the bottom edge to avoid too much rocker developing in the bottom.

Introducing a gentle 'S' shape into the side gives a flatter rocker in the bow section whilst producing a pronounced rocker into the after sections. Both features are desirable and produce a more sea-kindly shape.

Altering the shape of the side panels will have a fundamental effect on the curvature of the bottom of the hull.

form has the virtue of great simplicity, to the point that she can be built from a rough sketch without the need to make models or develop lines. Whereas once you start modifying the shape, then it is necessary to at least make a scale model beforehand.

Regardless of the details of bow and bottom edge, the transom should be set at a respectable angle which, if you are sufficiently bold, can be as great as 45°. The gunwale is left perfectly straight, and a far better appearance is achieved by giving the side panels an overall taper towards the stern.

Now, depending on the size of the sharpie and the thickness of the plywood being used, you may decide to add vertical timber frames which will increase the stiffness of the side panels and provide a location to the thwart risers, chine battens and inwales. The appearance of these frames is much improved if they are tapered slightly towards the gunwales. On a boat of around 16ft (4.8m), these frames can be placed at around 2ft (60cm) intervals.

STAGE TWO: BENDING THE SIDES

The sides must be bent around a central former so that they meet the stem and transom. When building with solid timber sides, the natural stiffness of the planks will ensure a smooth curve. Thinner plywood, on the other hand, can be rather 'wobbly', although this shortcoming can be resolved by screwing and gluing a gunwale batten along the outside of each panel. This will stiffen the panels considerably, so use relatively thin battens no more than ¾in (19mm) thick on a 16ft (4.8m) boat with a beam of 5ft (1.5m), and thinner on boats which are shorter with proportionately wider beams.

If we were to follow tradition, we would start this stage by attaching both sides to a pre-cut and shaped stem. The problem here is knowing the angle at which the sides meet at the bow so that the sides of the stem can be planed to the right bevel. The old sharpie builders knew the answer to this without drawing the lines, simply because they had done it before. We cannot draw on such experience, so must either set to work with pencil and battens and draw a plan view so that we can measure the angle, or find some other method of solving this problem.

One solution is to lash the central former in place, and using Spanish windlasses, gradually bend the bow and stern into position, temporarily inserting the transom blank to ensure that the right degree of curve is achieved. It is possible that intermediate cross-braces will also be needed to achieve the desired shape.

With the two sides of the bow pulled into place, our old friend the adjustable sliding bevel can be used to measure the angle. On a plumb-stern bow, the angle should be constant (or near enough so) from top and bottom – so check the angles at both ends. The stem can now be made, confident in the knowledge that when the sides are finally sprung round into their intended shape, it will fit perfectly.

Remove the Spanish windlasses and, if space allows, screw and glue the two side panels to the stem. However, have a 'dry run' first: this is perhaps the only stage where accuracy is really important, and you should be aiming to produce a perfectly equal V. The secret of success is for the front edges of the side panels to align perfectly with the stem piece. If this is not done accurately, the boat will adopt a natural twist that will be impossible to rectify.

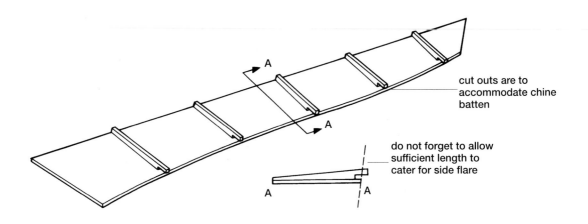

cut outs are to
accommodate chine
batten

do not forget to allow
sufficient length to
cater for side flare

An alternative to installing frames at a later stage; side frames can be installed
before the two sides are brought together.

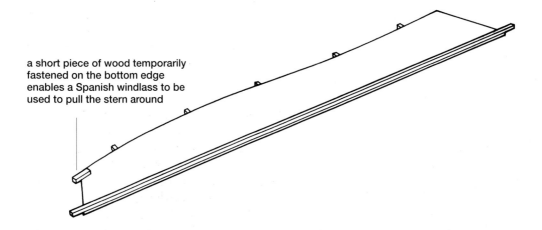

a short piece of wood temporarily
fastened on the bottom edge
enables a Spanish windlass to be
used to pull the stern around

Fastening the outer gunwale strake onto the plywood side before bending makes
the assembly less 'wobbly' and can result in a smoother curve. Extending the ends
beyond the side panel helps when bending the sides around the central former.

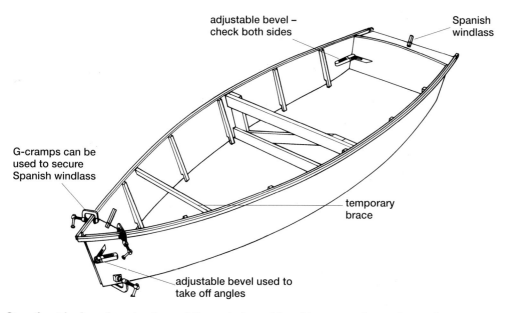

adjustable bevel –
check both sides

Spanish
windlass

G-cramps can be
used to secure
Spanish windlass

temporary
brace

adjustable bevel used to
take off angles

Once the sides have been bent round the central mould and temporary braces inserted to achieve the required shape, the angles between sides and transom and at the bow can be taken aft using an adjustable bevel gauge. The transom sides and the stem can be bevelled accordingly. Do not bring the stem to a point – leave a flat to take a capping strip.

If you have insufficient space to install the stem with the side panels spread out in a V, it is possible to first bend the panels round the amidships former, having already fitted the stem, dry, to each panel separately. But this requires even greater care to avoid building in a twist.

STAGE THREE: INSTALLING THE TRANSOM

The next task is to bend the sides fully round the amidships former or mould, and then to fit and install the transom. This is most easily done with the bottom uppermost because you will then have the advantage of gravity on your side, and you will have better access to measure the transom bevels.

One of the easiest ways of making the transom is to bend the sides in, using a pair of Spanish windlasses. Then measure the beam top and bottom, and the height, not forgetting to allow for a bold curve across the top, and the bevel at the bottom edge. Transfer the measurements onto the plywood, working about a centre line. Cut the plywood to shape, ignoring the bevels, and offer it into the gap. Bevels can then be directly measured using an adjustable bevel gauge. The plywood transom panel can be framed up using, typically, 3in by ¾in (76 by 19mm) thick timber, remembering to allow sufficient projection on the side and bottom edges to cater for the bevels.

With the timber frame glued and screwed to the plywood, cut the side bevels only, and glue and screw the transom in place. Work carefully, because this

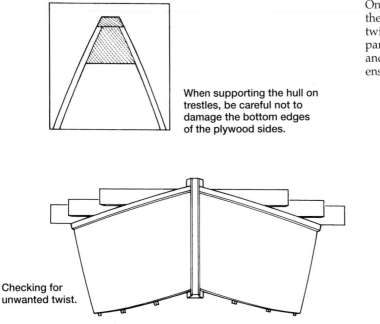

When supporting the hull on trestles, be careful not to damage the bottom edges of the plywood sides.

One method of checking that the hull is true and is not twisted is by placing a series of parallel bars across the gunwale and sighting over the top to ensure they are running true.

Checking for unwanted twist.

is another opportunity both to introduce twist and destroy symmetry.

STAGE FOUR: FITTING THE BOTTOM

Traditionalists may point out that planking athwartships – that is, the planks going across the boat, and not in line with the keel (as in the dory) – in fact defines a skiff. But we are building in modern materials so the bottom is being planked with plywood.

The first job is to install the chine battens, sometimes referred to as the chine logs. The problem here is that these battens are being fitted around an inside curve in between the stem and the transom. This is not as difficult as it may seem, although if you are at all unsure, cut a practice end using a short piece of scrap timber. Having

said that, where the end of the chine batten fits against either the stem or the transom frame, the angles are quite complicated and cannot be guessed. The solution is to transfer both the vertical and horizontal angles using the adjustable bevel gauge.

Start by offering up the battens, clamping them as you work outwards from a central position, and remembering to align the batten allowing sufficient overlap for it to be planed level across the bottom. If you have previously installed vertical frames with pre-cut lap joints, don't rely on these joints to hold the chines in place because this could split the frames at this point – use plenty of clamps.

Working on one side at a time, you should finish with the excess batten length sticking out at either end of the hull. A certain amount of judgement is now needed to decide exactly where to mark the angles for cutting, and it is preferable to err on the generous side and risk having to trim more off to achieve a perfect fit – always work to a marked line. Once one end fits accurately, the process is repeated at the other end.

Alternatively, it is possible to cheat by deliberately cutting the chine batten short of the transom and scarfing in a short closing piece after the main section of the batten is securely glued and screwed in place. Indeed, if the skiff has an exaggerated rocker, as is traditional on some designs,

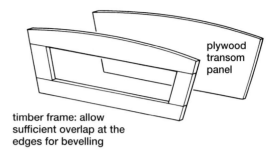

plywood transom panel

timber frame: allow sufficient overlap at the edges for bevelling

Basic plywood and frame transom construction

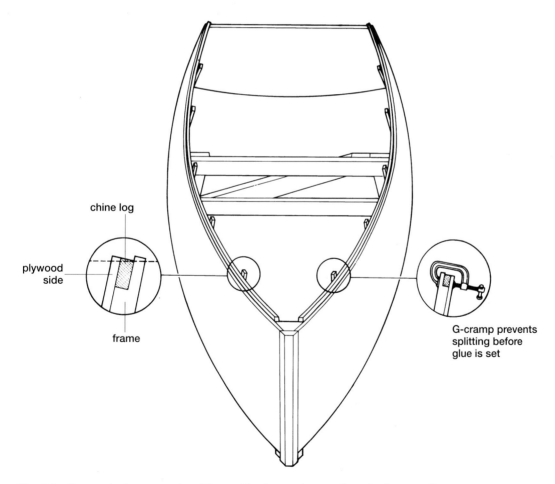

chine log

plywood side

frame

G-cramp prevents splitting before glue is set

The chine log can be bent round and located in the notches cut into the frame ends. It is a good idea to support the frame end with a G-cramp to prevent splitting.

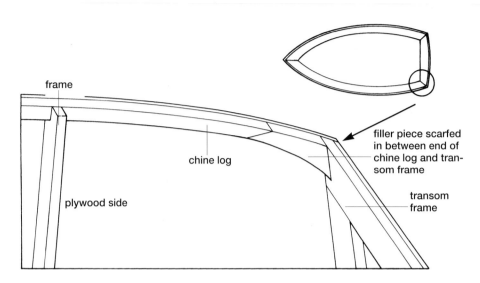

An alternative to fitting both ends of the log tight against stem post and transom is to stop it short at the transom end and close the gap by scarfing in a filler piece.

then it may be essential to adopt this technique in order to be able to force the chine batten into place round the tight curve. If the batten refuses to bend sufficiently, steaming could provide an answer; but perhaps a more practical approach is to put a narrow saw-cut down the length of the difficult bend – though be sure to drill a small hole at the end of the cut to prevent a split developing from this point.

Once both battens are in place and the glue has hardened, the bottom edges are then planed to take the bottom panel. Use a straight-edge to check the accuracy well before getting down to the final shaving so that any inaccuracy can be corrected in time, with wood to spare.

Once both chine battens have been bevelled, the bottom can be offered up: either join the sheets of plywood to make one complete bottom panel, or the bottom can be put on in sections. If a scarf joint is used,

it is perhaps better to joint the panel before offering it up in place. Butt joints, on the other hand, can be made in situ which for the single-handed builder has the advantage of making the panels easier to handle. Another advantage of fitting the bottom in sections is that it provides an easy check to verify whether or not the transom has gone in squarely.

Start by marking the centre line on the after panel before cutting it roughly to shape; this makes it easier to get the centre line absolutely square with the end that fits to the transom. Then cut the panel to shape leaving a good margin for trimming. Using sufficient screws to hold it firmly, attach the panel along the lower edge of the transom, making absolutely sure that the marked centre line coincides exactly with the transom centre line. Weight the panel so that it bends gently and rests snugly against the hull sides,

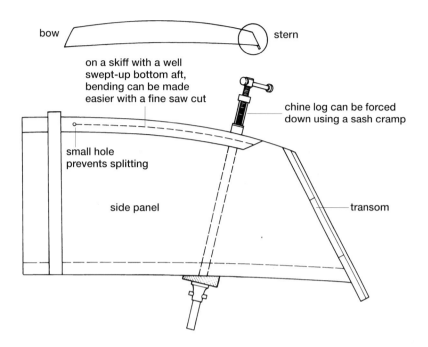

bow

stern

on a skiff with a well
swept-up bottom aft,
bending can be made
easier with a fine saw cut

chine log can be forced
down using a sash cramp

small hole
prevents splitting

side panel

transom

Using gentle force to persuade a reluctant chine log into place.

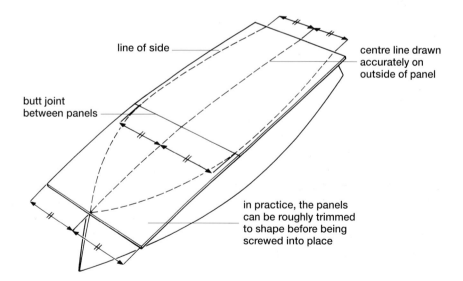

line of side

centre line drawn
accurately on
outside of panel

butt joint
between panels

in practice, the panels
can be roughly trimmed
to shape before being
screwed into place

Final check for symmetry: before gluing and screwing the bottom in place, offer up the panels, making absolutely sure the edge of the after panel lines up exactly with the transom, then measure from the centre line to the corners of the transom, about amidships and at the butt joint to make certain each side is equal. Also check that the centre line of the stem coincides exactly with that of the bottom panel. Any misalignment should be corrected.

taking up the rocker. Check that the centre line at the opposite end from the transom falls exactly equidistant between the two sides. If it doesn't, first try and find out why, and second, centralize the panel by sliding the forward edge sideways, then clamp it to the chine battens and carefully inspect and measure the hull to ensure that it has been pulled into line and has not simply been distorted further.

When it is clear that the hull is symmetrical, or at least as close as it is going to get, mark round the outside of the hull sides, remove the bottom panel, trim it to shape and then glue and screw it back into place. The forward panel can then be offered up, trimmed to shape and then glued and screwed into place. The butt strap can then be made and installed, ensuring that the glue has penetrated between the mating faces of the joint.

It is, of course, possible to use the same technique for checking the squareness of the transom when using a pre-scarfed bottom panel. Make sure that the centre of the stem coincides with that of the bottom panel when the sides are equally spaced from the centre line amidships and the transom is properly aligned. It provides less scope for triangulation but is still a valuable way of ensuring a symmetrical hull.

STAGE FIVE: COMPLETING THE GUNWALE

This stage involves installing the inner gunwale strakes, the chine rubbing strakes that not only protect the chine but also cap the exposed edge of the plywood bottom panel, and a keel and skeg. The inner gunwale strake can either be glued and screwed directly onto the inner face of the plywood, or stood off on small blocks placed at intervals of between 6in and 9in (15cm and 23cm) apart. This latter technique has many advantages, including greater rigidity with no increased weight, less chance of young crew members getting their fingers trapped between gunwale and quayside, and improved looks. It also gives a quick and easy emergency attachment point for lines.

The chine rubbing strakes can be relatively light in section, with well rounded outer corners. Alternatively, it is quite acceptable to reinforce the corner using 2in (5cm) woven glass tape and epoxy, in which case the corner between the bottom and sides should be very slightly rounded.

It may be convenient at this point to fit the keel and skeg, or this may be best left until later, depending whether or not transverse timber frames are to be fitted across the inside of the bottom.

Then follows the installation of thwarts and knees which I always consider to be one of the more interesting stages that turns a hull into a boat. The thwarts, or seats, can be straightforward planks of wood resting on risers either attached directly to the hull skin or set between the vertical frames. Alternatively you can fit enclosed buoyancy tanks that also form seats. This involves building in bulkheads up to seat level, then building a framework to support plywood tops. As we have already discussed, it is not a good idea to seal any area of a wooden boat; but this problem is easily overcome by installing watertight hatches, either panels screwed down on mastic or proprietary plastic hatches obtainable from chandlers. Details of fitting this type of seat are covered in the previous section.

Chine rubbing strakes –
alternatively, the corners
where plywood edges
need protecting can be
covered with glass tape
and epoxy.

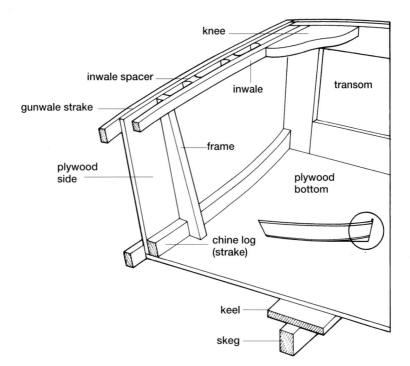

knee

inwale spacer

inwale

transom

gunwale strake

frame

plywood
side

plywood
bottom

chine log
(strake)

keel

skeg

Method of installing thwart (1).

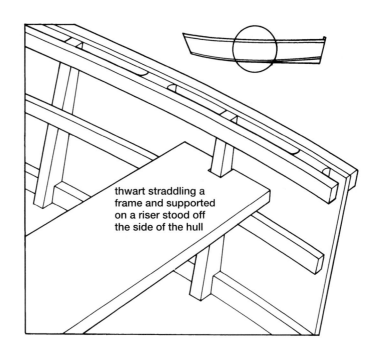

thwart straddling a
frame and supported
on a riser stood off
the side of the hull

107

thwart supported
on a riser attached
directly to the hull
side with the gun-
wale supported
by a knee

STAGE SIX:
PAINTING AND
INSTALLING FITTINGS

The final stage is to paint the boat and install fittings such as rowlocks and cleats, and perhaps to make a set of bottom boards both to protect the inside of the hull and to keep feet out of the bilge water.

Obviously this account is a simplified description, but it does contain all the major elements of building a simple flat-bottomed craft quickly and economically.

6 Plywood on Frame

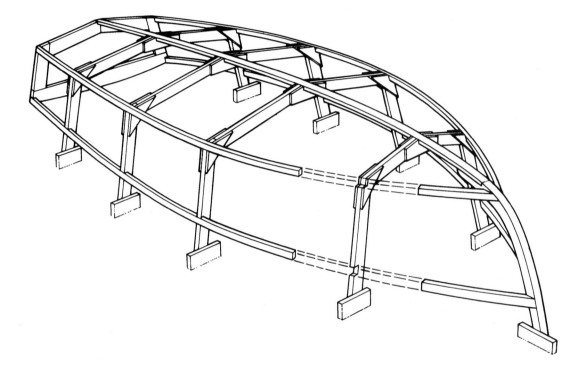

The main structure of a ply-on-frame boat is the frame which is glued and screwed together.

Before contemporary stitch-and-glue techniques were developed, plywood boats were invariably built over a timber frame that remained an integral part of the structure, and there are still many excellent plans available that employ this well tested method. And, although some might consider the technique somewhat outdated, it is far from obsolete and does in fact lead on to more professional methods of construction in general use today.

It is perfectly feasible for the amateur designer to create his own design to be built in plywood and timber-frame techniques, but it is somewhat more complex; therefore we will consider building from a proprietary set of plans. Unless the designer has supplied full-size patterns, it will be necessary to loft out the design before starting with tools and timber. (Lofting is covered in an earlier chapter, and involves making a full-size drawing of the hull.)

FRAME CONSTRUCTION

Once the lines have been faired and the exact shape of the frames established, frame-making can begin. The main thing to remember is that although you are building these frames from squared-off timber, when they are eventually set up on a floor or building horse, notches cut to accommodate chine and gunwale battens will have to be bevelled. This does not really affect the way in which you build the frames, but it does have a bearing on the way the separate pieces of timber are jointed, and also the way in which they are set up.

There is far less chance of an error being made if the frames are laid out directly on the lofted lines, but if this is not possible, the outside shape of each frame must be carefully reproduced on a stout sheet of block-

board or a building board constructed from solid timber.

Working from the full-size lofting, the straight sections of timber for making the frames can be laid out and the angles of the chine joints transferred directly onto the timber. You have a choice: either these corners are formed with butt joints reinforced with plywood gussets on both sides, or halving joints can be used. In favour of the former is that if the chines are screwed onto the frames (as is generally the case) the screws are very likely to locate right down the centre of the joint, which would be most unsatisfactory. Though not so aesthetically elegant, the stronger solution is to butt joint the chine angles and arrange them so that the wider faces of the chines are not located on sections of end grain.

When cutting the side members, remember to extend them down to the datum line rather than stop them short at gunwale level: this is so they can be set up on the building floor, keel uppermost. Assemble and glue each frame on the station drawing, first attaching the plywood corner gussets on one face, and then when the glue has set, turning them over and gluing the mating gussets on the other side.

At this point the hog-and-chine fitting can be anticipated by cutting the notches. But leave plenty of wood for the bevels, which must be planed after the frames have been set up. The next task is to make the stem, and depending on the designer's preference, it can be either laminated from thin strips of timber or made using a sandwich construction.

MAKING THE STEM

When building more than one boat, it is worth spending time and money on

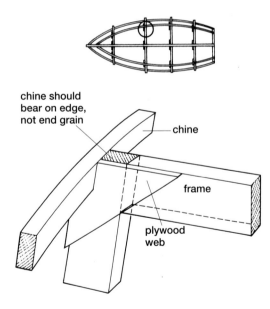

chine should bear on edge, not end grain

chine

frame

plywood web

This drawing highlights the truth about there being very few right angles on a boat. (The plywood web should always be made as large as possible.)

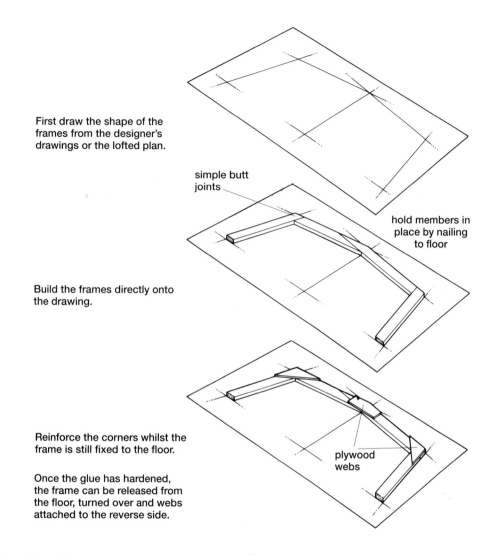

First draw the shape of the frames from the designer's drawings or the lofted plan.

simple butt joints

hold members in place by nailing to floor

Build the frames directly onto the drawing.

Reinforce the corners whilst the frame is still fixed to the floor.

Once the glue has hardened, the frame can be released from the floor, turned over and webs attached to the reverse side.

plywood webs

Three stages of making a frame.

sophisticated laminating jigs; however, when making only a single item from the jig, the more inventive you can be the better. A convex curve is needed, against which the strips of wood that will form the stem can be firmly clamped. Firm, even clamping is most important: there is nothing at all satisfactory about a piece of laminated timber with a thick, uneven glue line. For making the stem laminating jig, clipboard is a good choice. It is relatively inexpensive, you don't have to worry about the direction of the grain, and it is stable.

Cover the jig with polythene film to prevent the laminated timber bonding to the

Frames.

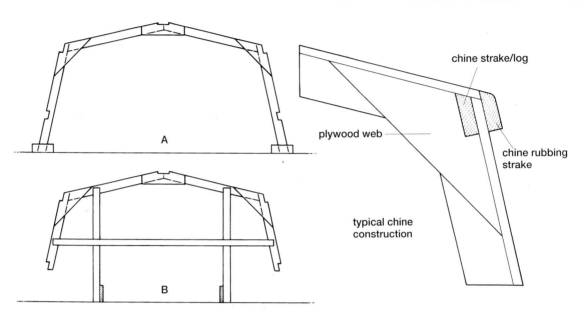

chine strake/log

plywood web

chine rubbing
strake

typical chine
construction

A

B

Two methods of supporting a frame:

A extends the sides down to the work base line.

B uses temporary battens to support the frame.

The chine at a much later stage – but keep construction detail in mind when setting up frames.

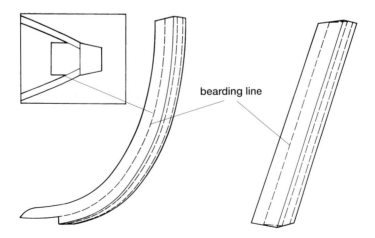

bearding line

Examples of curved and straight stems. The bearding line makes the inside of the bevel that must be cut to accommodate the angle of the planking.

jig though check with a test piece before committing yourself. I remember making a terrible mess with some plastic sheet that I thought was polythene but which turned out to be polyurethane instead.

A problem that can occur when clamping the strips in place is that individual pieces of timber slide sideways, relative to one another. This should not happen if each strip is perfectly parallel in cross-section, but if it does, light clamping pressure applied sideways can prevent it. An effective way to do this is to attach the jig to a base board, which can also be made from chipboard, so that clamping 'fingers' can be screwed down to hold the laminate pack in place.

Sandwich Construction

The alternative to laminating is sandwich construction using short lengths of timber with staggered butt joints. The aim is to arrange the lengths of each section so that the grain runs as near as possible round the bend of the stem. But avoid having too many butt joints – the greater the overlap between butt joints, the better. Once the blank for the stem has been constructed, the notch for the hog can be cut. It is also possible to fashion the bevel to take the plywood skin, transferring the bevels from the lofted lines. But if you are not sufficiently confident to do that,

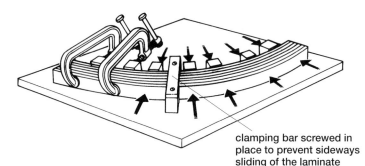

clamping bar screwed in place to prevent sideways sliding of the laminate

Building stem blanks. A stem can be laminated on a simple jig made from a board with blocks attached to form the curve.

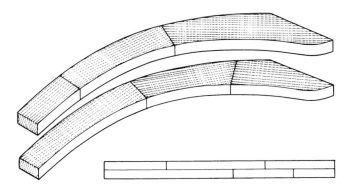

A straightforward way of avoiding cross-grain is to build the stem using sandwich technique and butt joints.

113

simply mark the bearding line – the inside line of the bevel – and also the centre line of the stem.

MAKING THE TRANSOM FRAME

Before setting up, we need to make the transom frame. The reason for leaving the frame in its unclad state is that it makes fitting the chine and gunwale battens far easier. The transom frame should be constructed by first making a Tee which will form the top and centre members. The leg of the Tee can be halving jointed into the top member, but with the joint only extending around two-thirds across its width; this will avoid having to deal with an end grain showing in the top of the finished transom

Once the Tee is complete, it can be presented to the full-size lofting of the transom and the remainder of the frame built around it, using either halving joints on the corners, or butt joints reinforced with plywood webs. Remember to include sufficient overlap to allow for the side bevel when fairing up to fir the plywood side and bottom panels.

The frames, stem and transom must now be set up accurately on the building floor. One of the most useful pieces of equipment to help with this is a large square. You can buy one at vast cost, or make your own using the three-four-five ratio sided right-angled triangle rule. Draw a 90° angle on the floor and build your square to that. Simple lap joints can be used for quickness, but if halving joints are used, the square is much handier.

SETTING UP

There are great similarities between setting up the frame and lofting out the original lines, the main difference being that setting up is a three-dimensional operation. However, the form is the same and it can be a great help to picture the lofted lines in your mind's eye. Start by laying down a centre line on the floor, and then draw in the frame stations using the home-made wooden square. (One of the most reliable methods of producing a straight line is to

A transom frame can be built using various forms of halving joints.

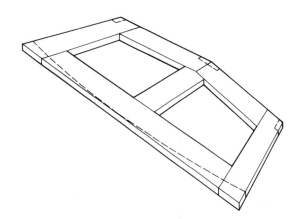

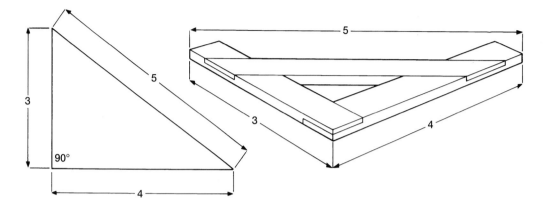

Making a square to the ratio of 3:4:5 from timber.

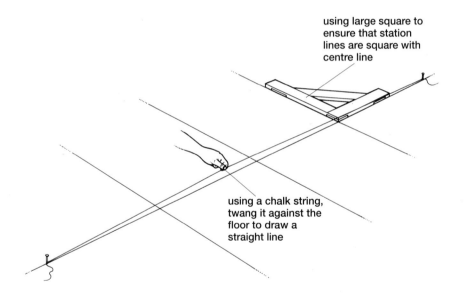

using large square to
ensure that station
lines are square with
centre line

using a chalk string,
twang it against the
floor to draw a
straight line

Marking out the floor in preparation of setting up the frame using a chalk line.

use a chalked string – as explained in an earlier chapter, this is an ordinary length of thin household string generously rubbed with chalk. Stretch it between two points across the floor and ping it like plucking a guitar string, and it will leave a straight chalk-dust line across the floor.)

If a flat wooden floor is not available, the boat will have to be set up on a strong-back, a stout timber frame with a central spine (preferably two pieces of timber set up side by side) and cross-members positioned to coincide with the frame stations. Rough or second-hand timber can be used, but don't skimp on size; a rockered hog and keel can impose quite a high degree of stress, and it is important that it is sufficiently rigid to resist bending. If the strongback can be bolted down to a solid floor, so much the better.

When setting up the frames, remember that the outer faces must be bevelled to the curve of the sides and bottom of the hull. This might sound obvious, but the consequences of lining them up on the wrong side of the line are problematic to say the least. Those forward of that central station should be placed forward of the station line, whilst those towards the stern should be placed on the transom side of the line.

Accuracy is important at this point, the critical factor being the relative position of the base line on the legs of each frame. This must be transferred directly from the full-size lofted frame drawings. If the hull is being set up as a strongback, the frame legs should extend beyond the base lines which can then be lined up with the top face of the strongback. But when setting up on a reliably flat floor, the frames can be trimmed off to the base line and stood directly down to the floor. On an uneven floor, it may be necessary to use levelling blocks, checking across the top faces with a spirit level. The tops of the blocks then become the base line drum.

This preliminary stage is completed by setting up the stem and transom. The important point here is to ensure that they are placed accurately and supported firmly. It is also vital to support all frames with fore-and-aft diagonal braces down onto the strongback.

FAIRING THE FRAME

Provided the frames are well braced, it is often far easier to fair the frames before fitting the hog and stringers. Placing a flexible batten over the frames will show the magnitude of the task, and also towards which side of the frames the bevels must be applied. It is, in fact, possible to mark planing lines by measuring the gap between frame and batten on the open side and transferring the measurement to the other side. But it is a good idea to do this in at least three points along the frame member, especially in the forward sections of the bottom where the panel can be tortured into a twisted form. But even when working to a line, which is very much recommended, it is important to check progress regularly to ensure that no mistakes are being made.

It is best to work round the frames progressively, taking a little of each at a time; don't attempt to complete the bevel on one frame before moving on to the next. And don't forget the stem: here, the bevel should be taken down to the bearding line, but this is where discretion must be used because it is more important to produce an even width along the front face of the stem than to adhere strictly to the bearding line – unless the design specifically calls for the stem to widen towards the top.

HOG, CHINES AND INWALES

The hog, or keelson as it is sometimes called, is the backbone of the hull; it should sit slightly proud of the frames to allow for bevelling to form lands for the bottom panels. But first the bottom of the frame joints into which the hog fits must be bevelled, and it is far easier to do this using a narrow batten to measure the bevel angles. First, gently clamp the batten in place across the frames in the prepared notches, and onto the stem. Measure the gap on the open sides of the joints, and transfer the

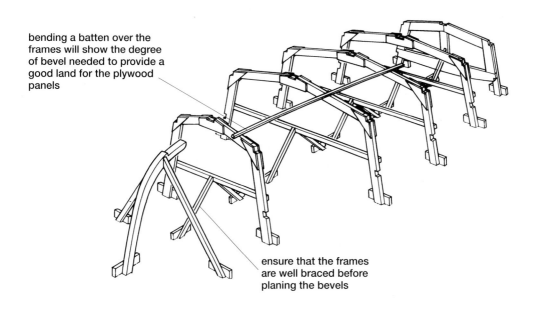

bending a batten over the frames will show the degree of bevel needed to provide a good land for the plywood panels

ensure that the frames are well braced before planing the bevels

Using a batten for fairing the frames.

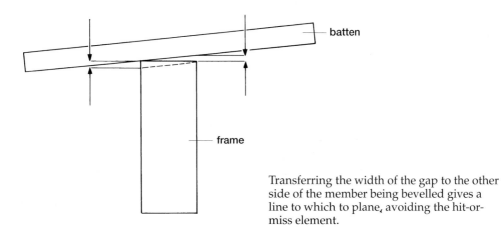

batten

frame

Transferring the width of the gap to the other side of the member being bevelled gives a line to which to plane, avoiding the hit-or-miss element.

dimensions onto the other sides of the frames. Extend the line across the full width of each joint in pencil, and then use a marking knife to finish off. Saw down to the line with a sloping cut and then remove the waste wood with a sharp chisel, working from the low side, chiselling up the slope of the bevel.

When all the frames, including the transom frame, have been bevelled thus, check

117

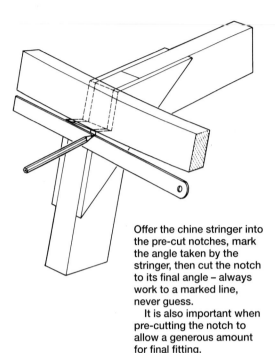

Offer the chine stringer into the pre-cut notches, mark the angle taken by the stringer, then cut the notch to its final angle – always work to a marked line, never guess.

It is also important when pre-cutting the notch to allow a generous amount for final fitting.

Chine stringer-to-frame joint.

each joint with the batten; if all is well, the hog can be glued and screwed into place. If the boat is to have a centreboard or dagger board, the slot may be cut before the hog is secured in place, or left until later. It all depends on the design instructions, but a strong case can be made for cutting the slot at a later stage, because if the slot is not pre-cut, the hog will bend more evenly over the frames.

The chines and inwales are fitted by the same technique of offering up the strakes to the squared-off joints, marking and cutting the various bevels. An added complication is fitting the stringers to the stem post so that it fits neatly to the bearding line. Fix them temporarily in place on the frames, and then bend each individual stringer to its position against the stem. Using a combination square – one with a sliding rule – strike a line square across the stringer from the bearding line and cut the stringer to length. Then with a

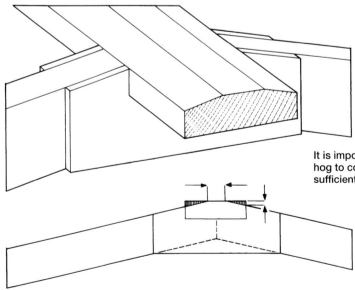

It is important to allow sufficient depth in the hog to combine the necessary keel width with sufficient land area for the bottom panels.

Hog (keelson) to frame joint on a Vee-bottomed hull.

Marking stringer to fit onto stem.

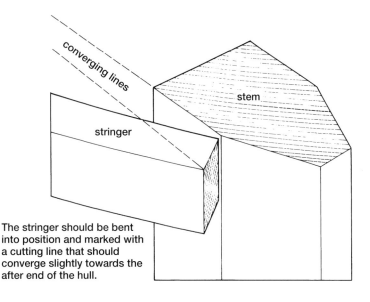

converging lines

stem

stringer

The stringer should be bent
into position and marked with
a cutting line that should
converge slightly towards the
after end of the hull.

straight-edge as a guide, mark a line across the stringer running almost parallel with the side of the stem, converging slightly towards the stern.

The wedge-shaped section must be removed from the stringer so that it will fit neatly against the stem. Simply marking a line parallel with the side of the stem will not do, because as the stringer is pushed in to make contact with its mating surface, a small gap will appear at the after end of the joint. This introduces an element of trial and error into the task; but by erring on the side of caution and fitting the stringer to the stem before the transom end is trimmed off, it is possible to have a second attempt by moving the stringer forward a little.

MORE FAIRING

The depth of bevel on the hog is determined by the angle and height of the frames in relation to the thickness and width of the hog, but it is a good idea at this point to check the plans to see how the keel is to be fitted. It may be that the keel should be fitted before the bottom panels, or the design may call for the apex formed by the angle between the two sides of the bottom to be planed flat and the keel simply glued and screwed on top. But whatever the detail of the hog and keel, the main aim at this point is to provide an adequately wide bearing surface for the plywood to form sound joints along the hog and stringers. And do not be seduced by the thought that provided epoxy is used to fill the gaps, an accurate fit doesn't really matter: such a philosophy leads to slovenly work, and also to increased cost – as it is, the glue in a boat can be a significant part of the overall cost; and if you use twice as much to fill unnecessary gaps, the cost of building it can be greatly increased.

The secret of successful fairing is to check progress regularly with a batten and a straight-edge. It is also a good plan to work towards pencil lines, thus avoiding

119

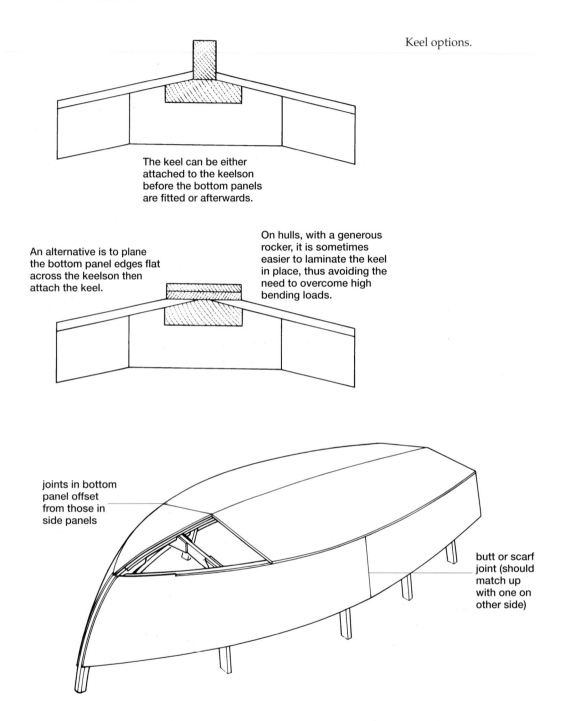

Keel options.

The keel can be either
attached to the keelson
before the bottom panels
are fitted or afterwards.

An alternative is to plane
the bottom panel edges flat
across the keelson then
attach the keel.

On hulls, with a generous
rocker, it is sometimes
easier to laminate the keel
in place, thus avoiding the
need to overcome high
bending loads.

joints in bottom
panel offset
from those in
side panels

butt or scarf
joint (should
match up
with one on
other side)

In this example which suggests a layout for the panels, the last section of panel is all
that remains, but first a butt strap must be put in place to form the bottom joint
between panels.

the risk of removing more valuable wood than you intended.

FITTING THE PANELS

If you are working to a designer's plan, it is likely that the dimensions for cutting the panels are given. But this is not necessarily the case, and it may be necessary to determine the panel shapes from the frame. Spending a little time to work out the most economical way the various panels can be cut from standard-size plywood can save a great deal of plywood. If working space is limited, or when developing complicated panel shapes, templates can be made from cheap hardboard instead.

Whichever method you choose, it is a relatively straightforward process to mark out the panel shapes directly from the frame structure. But it is important to remember to position the joints between the panels so that they don't line up, but are staggered from panel to panel. Additionally, the joints will look far better if balanced in pairs. It is also a sensible precaution to arrange the joints away from areas of high curvature, otherwise a ripple may be visible in the completed hull.

Deciding on Joints

Before marking out the panels you must also decide what type of joints are to be used between them. Scarf joints look best, but some designs lend themselves better to a combination of scarf and butt joints, with the latter being used in the bottom panels. The panel joints can be made

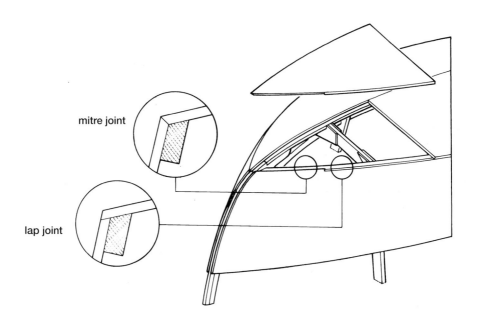

mitre joint

lap joint

Because of the shallow angle between panels towards the bow, it is sometimes necessary to change from a lap joint to a mitre joint. Installing the side panels first means that the stringer protecting the ply end-grain is on the side, not the bottom of the hull.

121

either before or after the panels are cut to shape. Usually it is more convenient to scarf the joints after the panels are cut from the sheet – allowing, of course, sufficient overlap to make the scarf. Marking out the panels can be as simple as laying the plywood in position over the framework and marking round with a pencil. Sometimes, however, it is not possible to get a pencil into the restricted space to draw in the outside line. The technique that must then be adopted is to draw round the inside of the frame and add on the width of the stringer.

Another feature that must be decided is the type of longitudinal joint to be made between panels, along the chines. When the panels meet at a shallow angle, the only solution may be to make a mitred butt joint; where they meet at a steep angle, it may be better to have one panel edge overlapping the other. Where the angle changes towards the bow, you may need to combine the two, with an overlap for the most part, converting into a butt joint at the bow section.

Protecting Plywood Edges

The important thing to remember is that the completed hull should not have exposed plywood edges because water will penetrate down the end grain and eventually cause delamination. There are a number of ways to avoid this trap, but perhaps the easiest being simply to glue a capping strip over the exposed edge. Another is to plane a flat across the corner, or to cut a rebate and glue on a capping piece that can be faired into the hull shape. A further method is to use epoxy and glass tape to cover the whole joint, much in the same way as stitch-and-glue construction, fairing the taped joint into the hull sides with filler.

The first solution has the advantage of simplicity and can also provide a good deal of protection to the chine. However, it can be criticized as being unattractive. The second solution requires more skill, especially when fairing the strip into the hull; over-enthusiastic work with the plane can inflict serious damage to the surface veneer of the plywood. The final solution, that of glass taping, is relatively simple, gives good protection to the chine but is difficult to execute well enough for a varnished finish.

Order of Fitting

If it has not already been done, start by fitting the transom panel; this way, the edges are automatically capped by the bottom and side panels. On most flat-panel hull forms when lap joints are used along the chines, it is usual to start panelling at the gunwale, working towards the keel. But if the bevelled butt joints are being used, it may be more convenient to start with the bottom panel, fitting the lower edge of the panel to the keel line first.

When the panel is scarfed to make up the length, it is good practice to have the outside edges of the joints trailing towards the stern; then should the boat be dragged over a spike or sharp stone, the joints are less likely to be caught up and damaged. So if the scarf joints have not already been made, start fitting the panel sections from the stern which allows the overlap to occur in this way. Temporarily fix the panels in place using steel screws; these are unlikely to break in the same way as bronze or brass, and will cut the thread in preparation for when the permanent screws are inserted.

If the panels have been fitted in sections, it is best to complete the scarf joint on the bench; but before removing the sections of

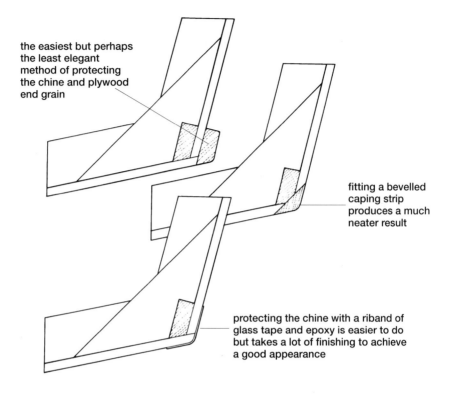

the easiest but perhaps the least elegant method of protecting the chine and plywood end grain

fitting a bevelled caping strip produces a much neater result

protecting the chine with a riband of glass tape and epoxy is easier to do but takes a lot of finishing to achieve a good appearance

Three methods of protecting the chine.

panel from the framework, take a straight-edge and draw a single line of perhaps a yard (metre) or more straddling the scarf. Measure two reference points along the line, giving a datum for lining up when finally positioning and gluing the scarf. Butt joints are, by nature, easier to line up, but if there is any doubt about being able to complete the joint accurately, leave suf-ficient material around the edges for fine fitting after the panel has been jointed.

Final Gluing and Screwing

When finally gluing and screwing the pan-els in place, the secret is preparation: have everything that may conceivably be needed to hand, including a spare screwdriver. Depending on the size of the panel and the glue being used, it may be necessary to spread the glue in two stages, particularly in the summer when curing times may be reduced because of high temperature. Offer up the panel 'dry' and drive sufficient screws to hold it securely in place; then remove it and, working methodically from one end, apply glue to just over half the framework. Then working from the centre of the panel towards the end of the boat, fas-ten the panel in place, making sure that the unglued end can be bent sufficiently away from the frame to allow the second half of the frame to be spread with glue. When the first end has been well screwed down, glue is then applied to the remainder of the area being panelled, and fastening once again continues from the centre towards the end.

Once a pair of panels has been attached to the frame, the excess glue removed and the glue allowed to harden, the edges can be faired to the stringers – if lap joints are being used – and the following panels fitted using the same technique.

Finishing Off

With all the panels glued and screwed in place, capping strips can be fitted and faired in, along with the keel (if it is not already in place), keel capping strip and gunwale rubbing strake.

The hull may now be released from the floor or building strongback, although before doing so it may be wise to install a temporary cross-brace or two between the gunwales, if not already fitted, to prevent any springing when extended feet of the frames are cut free.

Once the boat is turned the right way up, attention can be directed towards fitting out. The same techniques may be used as for the fitting out of the stitch-and-glue hull – although at this point, the hull will be much stiffer than its stitch-and-glue counterpart.

DECKING

Giving a small boat a deck brings both advantages and disadvantages. It can prevent large green waves finding their way into the bottom of the boat when venturing into less sheltered waters, and it can provide a protected area for stowing picnic baskets and spare clothing. However, a deck in a small, light boat adds weight where it is least wanted, since it raises the centre of gravity of the hull, making it less inherently stable. The extra weight also reduces the boat's ability to rise over a big wave, and this in turn increases the likelihood of shipping it on board.

Therefore, if a boat is to be fitted with a deck, it must be light yet strong: light, to minimize the weight penalty; and strong, not only to withstand the flexing stresses imposed both when sailing and when being manhandled ashore, but also to take the impact of someone sitting or even standing on it. This means a laminated deck beams (or a combination of solid timber and laminated beams) possibly dovetailed into the inwales, together with a king plank which is a central spine, and perhaps bulkheads. On dinghies and dayboats, it may well be worth considering laminating the beams from alternate layers of a spruce and a mahogany to combine strength with lightness.

The important thing is to keep the shape of the deck simple. We have all admired those wonderful curves on the decks of Dutch sailing boats: in fact they are not as complicated as they may appear, but they are still far beyond the capabilities of most newcomers to boat building. The golden rule is to avoid trying to curve the plywood in two directions at once. It may be that a certain amount of compound curve cannot be avoided, but don't set out to make it more complicated than needs be.

Achieving an Even Curve

For a deck to look good, it is important to achieve an even curve without creating flats or a hump in the middle; this is done by a simple method of projection as illustrated in the diagram. The height, or crown of the camber depends on a number of factors, two of the main ones on a small boat being the amount of sheer and the

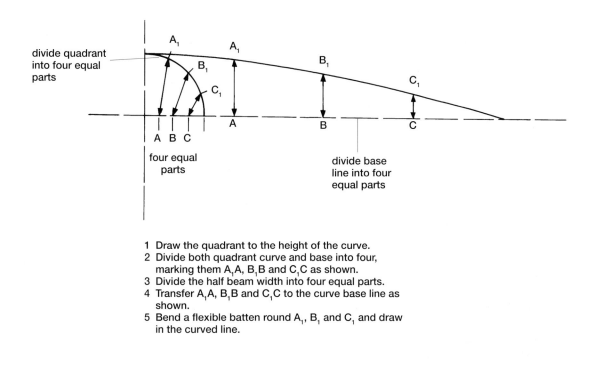

divide quadrant into four equal parts

four equal parts

divide base line into four equal parts

1 Draw the quadrant to the height of the curve.
2 Divide both quadrant curve and base into four, marking them A_1A, B_1B and C_1C as shown.
3 Divide the half beam width into four equal parts.
4 Transfer A_1A, B_1B and C_1C to the curve base line as shown.
5 Bend a flexible batten round A_1, B_1 and C_1 and draw in the curved line.

Drawing the camber on a beam given the height and width (beam).

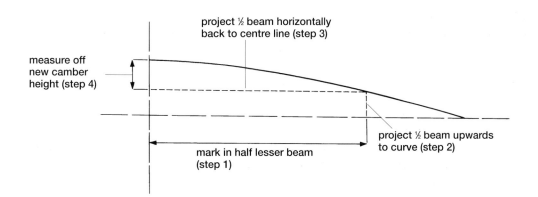

measure off new camber height (step 4)

project ½ beam horizontally back to centre line (step 3)

project ½ beam upwards to curve (step 2)

mark in half lesser beam (step 1)

Determining camber height of a lesser beam from a maximum beam curve.

The king plank can be dovetailed into the main deck beam or set in a cleat attached to the face of the beam.

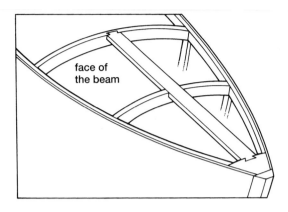

face of the beam

When letting the king plank into the beams, allowance should be made for curve across the top to produce a smooth camber.

angle of the deck from the stemhead. It is perhaps most convenient to generate the curve on a template that can be transferred to the actual beams.

The generally accepted method of creating a fair curve is as follows: measure out the maximum beam across which the curve is to span, then divide it in two to locate the centre. With a compass, draw a quadrant to the height of the camber. Now divide the perimeter of the quadrant into a number of equal parts – depending on the scale of the curve, this can be from four to six divisions. Divide the base of the quadrant into the same number of divisions; number these points A–A1, B–B1, C–C1, and link the points as shown on the diagram.

Now divide the half-beam base line into the same number of parts, and draw vertical lines from these horizontal divisions. Transfer dimensions A–A1, B–B1, C–C1 and so on, to the vertical lines drawn along the base line. This will generate a series of points which when joined using a flexible batten, will produce a fair curve without

humps or bumps. This curve can also be used to establish the crown heights of lesser beams on the same camber.

The danger with this type of joint is that it can take too much out of the inwale.

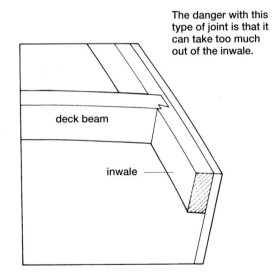

deck beam

inwale

It is possible to use a simple halving joint to lap the deck beams into the inwall but introducing a dovetail not only holds the gunwales apart but also prevents them from splaying. To work, the faces of the dovetail must be vertical.

Draw a horizontal line to pass through the curve at a point exactly equivalent to half the lesser beam, measured from the centre line. The distance that line is situated below the crown of the camber represents the new crown dimension.

All of this sounds very complicated, but it should become clear when considered in conjunction with the drawing.

Jointing the Beams into the Inwales

Jointing the ends of the beams into the inwales is perhaps a little more complicated than one might at first have imagined – it all stems from that old perennial problem of nothing on a boat being square. But with careful planning and marking out,

they can be fitted accurately without resorting to trial-and-error techniques: position the beam over the gunwales with a little spare length extending out over both sides and with the top edge parallel with the horizontal line of the deck. Mark the width of the beam across the inwale, and project the lines down the inside face. Then project perpendiculars up from the corners of the inwale, up both forward and after faces of the beam. It will then be clear how, by drawing in diagonals between the pairs of perpendiculars, the male parts of the joints can be drawn in.

Using dovetail joints on the beam ends is an effective method of ensuring that they prevent the gunwale spreading outwards, but only if they can be incorporated in such a way as not to significantly reduce the overall strength of the beam and inwale.

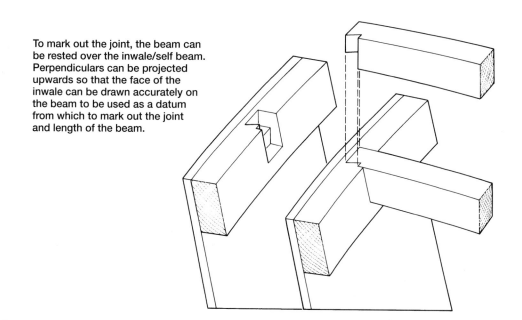

To mark out the joint, the beam can be rested over the inwale/self beam. Perpendiculars can be projected upwards so that the face of the inwale can be drawn accurately on the beam to be used as a datum from which to mark out the joint and length of the beam.

Beam into inwale joint.

Side Decks

Although some class dinghies have wide side decks, those on most general-purpose dinghies and dayboats tend to be quite narrow, and this requires a slightly different approach. Both, however, share a common component known as carling, or carline, a longitudinal timber that forms the inner edge of the side-deck framework. When the side decks are relatively narrow, the carlings can be supported away from the inwale on chocks, the spacing of which will depend on the degree of curve taken by the gunwale. On a short boat with a wide beam, it will probably be necessary to curve the chocks to match the curve of the inwale.

On wider side decks, the carlings are supported by half beams which are short deck beams. They are jointed into the carlings using the same type of joint as is used to fasten the beams to the inwales.

In theory, building side decks is very straightforward, because they are simply an extension of the foredeck taken back towards the stern and perhaps meeting up with an after deck. However, the geometry is not always straightforward, and although it may seem at first that the simplest form is one with a straight carling, picture the sheer line and you will soon realize that what might seem like a straight carling is far from being so. Geometrically, the simplest solution is to have a curved carling that runs parallel or nearly so with the gunwale; it may not naturally follow the exact deck camber, but on a small boat it will probably be near enough for practical purposes.

Such carlings can be laminated from relatively thick timber, then temporarily supported by dummy cross-beams clamped

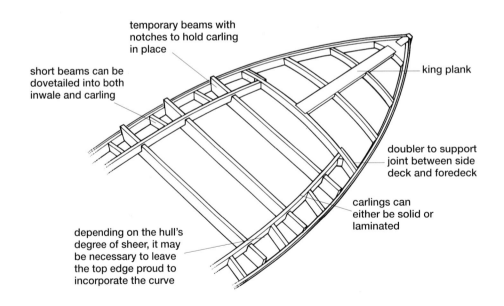

temporary beams with notches to hold carling in place

short beams can be dovetailed into both inwale and carling

king plank

doubler to support joint between side deck and foredeck

carlings can either be solid or laminated

depending on the hull's degree of sheer, it may be necessary to leave the top edge proud to incorporate the curve

Holding the carlings with temporary beams.

DECKING OPTIONS

The Plywood Deck

into place across the frames. They should have the same camber as the full deck beams, and have notches cut to receive the carlings which are jointed, at one end into the after foredeck beam, and at the other into either the transom or the forward after deck beam – again, using joints similar to those used between deck beams and inwales.

If the deck is to support a mast, then the beams that straddle the mast position may be strengthened with knees to spread the load into the hull more evenly. When the mast is keel-stepped – with the foot of the mast bearing onto the hog or keelson – a mast chock will be set between the two adjacent beams, using dovetailed joints to prevent the beams spreading. If deck-stepped, the deck will need supporting either by a bulkhead or a mast strut, positioned directly beneath the mast station.

Although some of the more expensive small wooden boats had laid decks similar to those found in larger yachts, many small dayboats were decked using tongue-and-groove boarding covered with painted canvas. However, with the advent of marine plywood, all the problems of planked decks were solved at a stroke. Perhaps the most obvious advantage of a deck covered in ply is the inherent lack of leaks. But lightness runs a close second, and it could be argued that on a dayboat, lightness is a more important than the odd small leak. Moreover as far as the builder is concerned, plywood decking is perhaps the quickest and easiest to construct. It is mainly a matter of

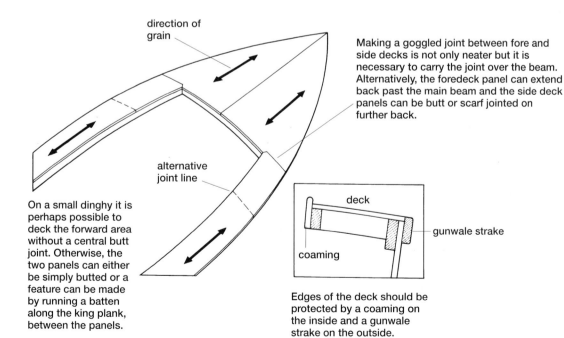

direction of grain

Making a goggled joint between fore and side decks is not only neater but it is necessary to carry the joint over the beam. Alternatively, the foredeck panel can extend back past the main beam and the side deck panels can be butt or scarf jointed on further back.

alternative joint line

On a small dinghy it is perhaps possible to deck the forward area without a central butt joint. Otherwise, the two panels can either be simply butted or a feature can be made by running a batten along the king plank, between the panels.

deck

coaming

gunwale strake

Edges of the deck should be protected by a coaming on the inside and a gunwale strake on the outside.

Plywood deck panel layout.

thorough planning and an eye for grain patterns, because a more satisfactory result is achieved if the grain runs parallel with the fore-and-aft centre line or the sides of the hull. This can result in somewhat uneconomical use of the plywood, especially when joining the side decks to the fore-and-aft decks, but the slight increase in cost is worthwhile because on a small boat, the deck is often the most looked-at feature.

The thickness of plywood depends on several factors, including whether or not the deck will be stepped upon, the spacing of the deck beams and the degree of camber. The compromise is between weight and strength, and it is only too easy to affect the stability of a hull adversely by adding a heavy deck.

Fastenings

Because a deck is an aesthetic feature as well as a practical part of the boat, be sure that the fastenings used do not mar its appearance. Glue the deck in place using as few fastenings as possible, and remove these once the glue has set. On lightweight decking, temporary fastenings can include staples fired into the ply through a stout fabric ribbon which aids subsequent removal. On heavier decking screws will have to be used to provide sufficient strength to hold the plywood in place during gluing, but these can subsequently be removed and the holes plugged with matching timber dowels.

Simple Laid Deck

Plywood is not always appropriate, in which case one of the more traditional forms of decking may be chosen. Perhaps the most straightforward of these is the simple laid deck with cotton-caulked seams, fixed down with counterbored screws driven in from above, the screw holes being stopped with timber dowels.

A variation on this is to cut squared caulking grooves and caulk them with a modern synthetic compound; this fills the gap, making the decking watertight, and it also has adhesive qualities that glue the deck strips together whilst retaining a degree of flexibility.

Another variation is to secret-nail the planks of timber to the deck beams. This has the great advantage of hiding the fastenings which are driven at an angle (skew-nailed) through the edges of the strips, into the beams. To prevent unevenness it is also necessary to edge-dowel or edge-nail the planks to prevent the edges opposite the secret nails from lifting.

For simplicity these deck planks can be straight, running in line with the keel and taken right out to the edge, with the gunwale rubbing strake acting as a capping. For a professional job, however, the deck planking is curved to reflect the sweep of the gunwale; it should be notched into a king plank along the centre of the deck, and fitted with a covering board around the gunwale. This is a wider plank that forms a margin around the deck, both enhancing its appearance and providing better protection to the gunwale. On small boats, however, curving the deck planking can appear ostentatious but combining a straight deck planking with nicely curved covering boards provides a happy balance.

Tongue-and-groove Planking

Another interesting variation is splined or tongue-and-groove planking, with its seams glued to make it watertight. Again, secret-nailing can be used, although the

timber strips glued
in place with the
seams fitted with
marine sealer

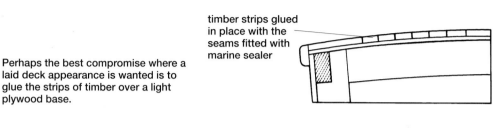

Perhaps the best compromise where a
laid deck appearance is wanted is to
glue the strips of timber over a light
plywood base.

stretched on
canvas bedded in
paint

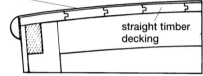

straight timber
decking

Traditional deck of tongue-and-groove
planking covered by painted canvas.

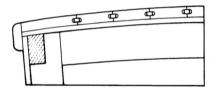

Splined deck in which both edges of the
deck planking is grooved and a timber
tongue prevents movement between
planks.

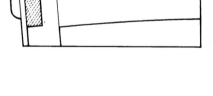

Traditional laid deck with caulked seams.
On smaller boats the seams can be
supported either by battens or dowels
between planks. This is not really suitable
for small boats.

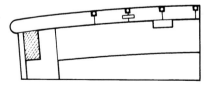

A modern version of a laid deck where
marine sealant is used in place of the
cotton caulking. Again this is not suitable
for small dinghies.

Traditional methods of constructing a deck. These are only suitable for larger boats
because of their weight.

splines or tongues obviate the need for dowels or cross-nailing. The disadvantage of a deck with glued seams, however, is that severe drying out can cause cracking.

Combining Plywood and Laid Timber Planking

A further option is to combine the advantages of plywood decking with the aesthetics of laid timber planking. The plywood can be glued and nailed onto the deck beams, and the planking laid directly on top. On the deck of a larger boat the planking can be glued and screwed from beneath, whilst that on smaller, lighter boats can be temporarily held in place whilst the glue is setting with tacks or staples that are later removed.

CENTREBOARDS AND DAGGERBOARDS

The difference between a centreboard and a daggerboard is this: a centreboard is housed in a box just forward of amidships, and pivots down, usually held in place by a bolt; a daggerboard also extends down through a box built into the keel/keelson, but it slides down into place and is not permanently attached to the boat. Both are intended to reduce sideways drift when the boat is sailing, and their position in it is relatively critical, creating a balance between hull and sails. I will assume, therefore, that anyone building a boat with either a centreboard or a daggerboard is working to a bought design – although it is not difficult for those with a working knowledge of small boats to work out where these should go. And quite often, other factors such as the thwart position dictate where they can be positioned. Traditionally the box would be made of relatively stout timber and either bolted or screwed into place, on a bed of mastic to make the seal watertight. In more recent time with boats built in plywood and epoxy, however, there is not such a pressing need to accommodate movement within the hull, so it is possible to glue the box in place.

Basically the box comprises two sides, usually made from ⅜in (10mm) ply, a front and a rear formed by a pair of timber battens which extend below the sides to the depth of the keelson, and two lengths of timber attached close to the bottom of the side panels to form a flange onto the keelson. Usually the box is mounted directly onto the keelson centre line, but there is a good argument for siting it to one side, as this avoids compromising the strength of the keel and keelson due to the slot. Either way, it is important to support the box with knees, or by linking the top of the box to a thwart.

7 Glued Lapstrake

This form of boat building was a direct result of the development of marine plywood; it is also considerably boosted by the introduction of epoxy adhesives. It goes under the name of glued clinker, too, although some argue that the term is a contradiction: the word 'clinker' derives from 'clench' which is a form of fastening, and in glued clinker there are no fastenings between the strakes, only glue. However, there is a further reason for calling it glued lapstrake. Clinker-building is usually associated with relatively narrow planking, whilst the strakes used on, for example, Iain Oughtred's 19ft (5.7m) *Caledonia Yawl*, Laurent Giles's 16ft (4.8m) *Jollyboat* and John Watkinson's *Drascombe Range* all have broad strakes and would be extremely difficult to build using traditional clinker-building techniques.

So what is 'glued lapstrake'? Quite simply, it is a form of construction in which the strakes are lapped over one another along their seams and fastened with a modern marine-grade glue, usually, but not exclusively, epoxy. Some might question the difference between multi-chine construction and lapstrake: the simple answer is, when the strakes are stepped in the same way as a traditional clinker hull the boat is lapstrake, and when the edges of the strakes are finished fair, the hull is multi-chined. Further, if the seams between the strakes are backed by stringers this is invariably multi-chine. Sometimes the joint is both stepped and has a stringer: however, stringers are usually only used in this way

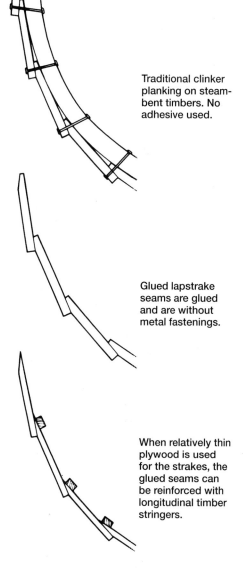

Traditional clinker planking on steam-bent timbers. No adhesive used.

Glued lapstrake seams are glued and are without metal fastenings.

When relatively thin plywood is used for the strakes, the glued seams can be reinforced with longitudinal timber stringers.

The difference between new and old.

when the strakes are not thick enough to allow a landing to be worked into the edge of the strake.

SETTING UP THE FRAMEWORK

So far we have considered building methods which have been economical in terms of building jigs: either the temporary framework has been minimal, as in the case of the skiff featured earlier, or the frame has become an integral part of the finished boat. One of the drawbacks of glued lapstrake is that it often demands a more complex, and therefore more expensive building frame. However, if you are building just one boat, cheap or second-hand materials may be used – provided they can be worked to fine tolerances. Having said that, if the framework is to become a permanent part of the hull, as is more often the case when building boats with broader strakes, it is simply not worth using second-class timber. The amount of time and care that will be spent on such a boat will justify using the best grade of timber your pocket will stretch to.

But back to basics once more, although we have now moved on from the simple hull from where the builder can allow the shape of the panels to affect the final shape of the hull. On boats with only two panels/strakes per side, there is little accumulated error should the shape of the panels not be quite accurate: provided each pair of panels is the same, the hull should come out symmetrical. However, where the boat has perhaps four, five or maybe more strakes per side, inaccuracies must not be allowed to build up and distort the hull.

The key to success is care in both the making and the setting up of the framework, and in accurately striking off the shapes of the strakes. Both framework and strakes have to be in sympathy, meaning that the strake must lie easily over the framework without creating any undue stress. As before, you start with the design, and at this level that would probably be a proprietary stock design. If it does not include full-size patterns of the frames, the lines will need to be lofted in the way described earlier; this will provide an accurate full-size drawing of the frames, stem and transom. If you are sufficiently experienced in the art of lifting, you will also be able to draw out the bevels. Depending on the curvature and complexity of the permanent frames, they can either be fabricated or – far better, but perhaps more labour-intensive – they can be made by laminating blanks over a simple laminating jig. The advantage of the latter type of frame is that it not only looks better but is usually, weight-for-weight, stronger than its built-up counterparts.

Depending on the size of the hull and the degree of complexity of its form, the plans may call for a combination of temporary and permanent frames. The temporary frames can be made from either scrap timber, cheap plywood or chipboard. A point to remember: it must be possible to remove temporary frames from the completed hull. It may, therefore, be necessary to make them in sections that can be taken apart.

Permanent Frames

Permanent frames will either be built up from sections of solid timber, or they will be laminated; it really depends on the shape of the hull as to which is the most practical. However, laminated frames usually look

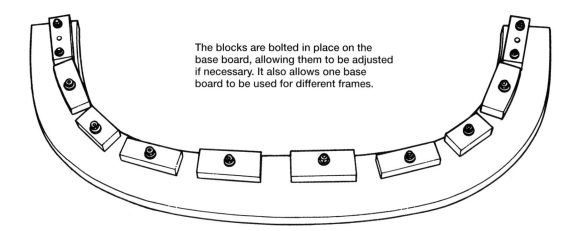

The blocks are bolted in place on the base board, allowing them to be adjusted if necessary. It also allows one base board to be used for different frames.

Typical laminating jig made from second-hand timber.

Whilst the inside of the laminated frame makes a smooth curve, the outside has to be bevelled to fit snugly to the planking. The variation in frame width should be accounted for when laminating the blank.

Section through a round-bottomed hull showing the frame fitted to the planking. On a traditional clinker hull the frame (timber) would not be notched into the planking and it would be riveted not glued in place.

much better, and are probably stronger, with a better strength-to-weight ratio. And provided they are made up of sufficient strips – each no more than ⅛in (3mm) thick – the frame should not spring when released from its former.

The technique for building frames from solid timber has already been covered, and that for laminating frames is basically the same as for laminating a stem. Built-up frames should be constructed directly from the lofted lines, taking care to make allowance for bevelling. Either halving or butt joints can be used. However, making halving joints between pieces of wood which come together at shallow angles can present a challenge. The advantage is that, unlike butt joints, halving joints don't usually require reinforcing with plywood gussets.

Although aesthetically they are far better, laminated frames are time-consuming to build, and if only one boat is being constructed, it can be expensive in terms of laminating jigs since each frame in the boat will require its own jig. Nevertheless, with careful planning a set of laminating jigs can be made relatively economically, and the rewards in terms of quality and appearance are usually handsome.

The lamination jig should be made using the details taken directly from the lines drawing. If the hull has relatively wide strakes, the series of flats that make up the shape of the hull must be converted into a nice sympathetic curve so that the laminates take a natural bend. If the transition is too severe, filler pieces can be added to the laminated blank to build up the outer contour.

It is often easier to laminate around the outside of a curve (with the former on the inside), so when making a former, the width of the frame must be taken into account.

MAKING THE STEM AND TRANSOM

When the frames are completed, the stem and transom can be made. Here again, the stem may be built up either by using the sandwich construction, or by scarfing short sections to produce the curve, or it can be laminated using the same techniques adopted for making the frames. If the

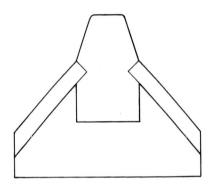

Traditional stem where strakes are set into a rabbet pre-cut into the one-piece stem.

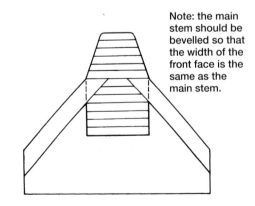

Note: the main stem should be bevelled so that the width of the front face is the same as the main stem.

A more modern approach where the stem is laminated in two pieces with the outer capping piece glued in place after the planking has been done.

builder is left to decide on the frame and stem construction, the strong argument for laminating is timber stability, which is more in keeping with the requirements of a glued lapstrake than a solid timber built-up stem which is subject to greater dimensional changes with varying moisture content.

When planking a traditional clinker hull, it is usual to cut rabbets (Vee-shaped grooves) in the sides of the stem into which the ends of the planks will fit. This demands a good deal of painstaking work which, if glued lapstrake construction is combined with a laminated stem, can be avoided. The alternative is to bevel the stem and, once the planking is in place, continue building up the front of the stem with further laminations to form an outer, false stem. But if the stem is to look right, the geometry must be the same as that of a traditional rabbeted stem.

The transom is another example where glued lapstrake varies from traditional clinker construction. A traditionally built boat would have a solid timber transom, whilst that of a glued-lapstrake boat is more likely to have a plywood transom reinforced with a timber frame.

SETTING UP THE HULL

Unlike conventional clinker construction where the hull is usually planked the right way up, glued lapstrake hulls are more conveniently planked upside-down. It is easier that way because it gives better access for bevelling the strake lands; it also makes clamping easier. As with a conventionally framed plywood construction, the frames are either set up on a wooden floor, or on a timber strongback. Here again, a great deal of care and attention should be directed towards ensuring that they are set

up accurately, and are squarely and correctly spaced. Depending on the size and design of the boat, the frame may need varying degrees of support, ranging from a couple of temporary vertical struts, to a complete mould-shaped backing support onto which the frames are temporarily attached. For economy, always try to use second-hand timber, but *don't* compromise on accuracy.

The frames are followed by the stem and transom, then the hog or keelson which must fit snugly into notches cut along the centre line of the frames, and with sufficient protrusion to allow for fairing. The depth to which the keelson is let into the frames is relatively critical, and is therefore worth first drawing out on the lofted lines.

Fairing the frames, transom and keelson is straightforward, requiring a sharp plane and long flexible batten. Planing the bevel on the stem demands a little more attention to detail to ensure that the outer or false stem, which will be installed after the planking is complete, looks right.

Once again, back to the lofted lines. The aim is to predict the width of the flat running up the front of the stem from the forefoot to the stem head, which should be parallel. This may seem a very simple task at first – just bevel the stem leaving a parallel flat up its entire length. But whilst this may be so with some hull forms, it is likely that the angle at which the planking joins the stem will vary from top to bottom. In this case, making the leading edge of the stem the same width for its entire length would probably result in narrowing stem width, as the angle of the planking to the stem becomes finer towards its forefoot.

So, back to the lofted lines, and at various points up the stem, draw lines at right-angles to the tangent of the stem's curve. Then project the angle and thickness of the

The aim is to develop the angle seen at right angles to the tangent of the stem curve taking the joint between strakes as a reference.

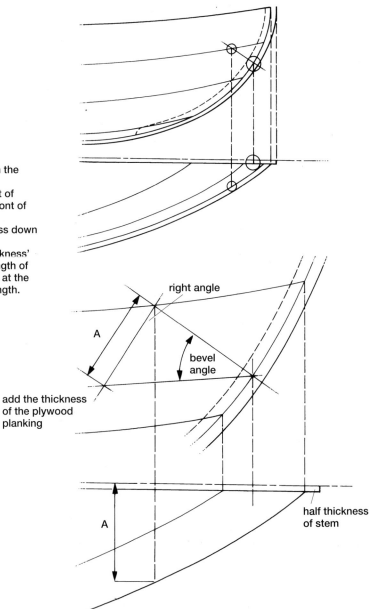

Remember:

1 Lofted lines drawings are made from the inside of the hull planking.
2 Use the edge of the hood ends (front of planking) in the projection, not the front of the stem.
3 The bevel will change as you progress down the stem towards the hog.
4 The aim is to maintain the 'stem thickness' over the planking, right along the length of the stem so that the width of the flat at the front of the stem will vary over its length.

right angle

A

bevel angle

add the thickness of the plywood planking

half thickness of stem

A

Establishing bevel along a stem.

converging planking, drawing a section of the stem to show the bevel angle. All this sounds very complicated, but it is in fact very simple when considered in conjunction with the accompanying illustration.

Once determined, the dimensions for the front face of the stem can be transferred onto the stem, measuring outwards from the centre line. The bevel can be planed into the stem using angles transferred from the lines lofting. However, the amateur will probably find it easier to cut the stem bevels, bending a batten round the frames as a guide. One pitfall is to forget to stop the bevel at the top edge of the sheer strake. Stopping the bevel creates a shoulder, thus providing a positive reference so that both sheer strakes finish at the same level; it also improves the detailing possibilities for the stem head.

The bevel along the keelson also needs to be planed at this point. Again, the angles could be lifted from the lines lofting, but it is far more straightforward to bend a thin batten around the frame, along a line to coincide with the top edge of the garboard, and gauge the bevel from it using a steel rule spanning from the batten to the keelson. The golden rule is never guess a bevel angle: always use some form of reference in the form of a straight-edge, a flexible batten or a bevel gauge.

PLANKING

Each strake has to be marked out, cut to size, scarfed, fitted, rebated and bevelled, and finally fastened in place. The success of each stage depends on the care taken over the previous task; but approached methodically, there are no hidden pitfalls. However, before starting to concentrate on marrying strakes to framework, a little

thought must be given to the plywood itself. Unless the boat is less than 8ft (2.4m) long, or you are prepared to spend a lot of money on non-standard sheet sizes, you will have to think about scarfing sheets to achieve the lengths needed. Scarfing has already been covered, but what you have to decide on is when to make the scarf: is it better to scarf a number of lengths of ply together *before* marking out and cutting to size, or is it better to fit the strake in sections, scarfing them together once a reasonably good fit has been achieved? The answer depends on the shape of the strake, its length, and the facilities for handling and working a long, narrow piece of plywood.

Probably the most convenient approach is to scarf the sections together before shaping, and on a hull that has relatively straight strakes this is perfectly feasible without creating too much waste. On strakes of over 16ft (4.8m), however, it may be more practical to mark out and cut the sections separately, and then to make the scarf joints. The problem is that the scarf may occur at a curved section of the strake, making it difficult to align the joint, and the scarf must be gauged to end up with a strake of exactly the right length. This may sound fraught with problems, but two simple steps can make it relatively easy.

First, each section of the strake must be made slightly longer to allow for making the scarf joint plus a little waste for trimming. Fit each section separately, remembering to pencil a mark on each to coincide with a frame so that they can be replaced accurately. Replace a mating pair with the ends overlapping. Now mark in the width of the scarf across the edges of the strake, making two tick marks on each edge. Without moving the sections, draw a straight line along the strake across the scarf joint. To make this easier, use a spare length of

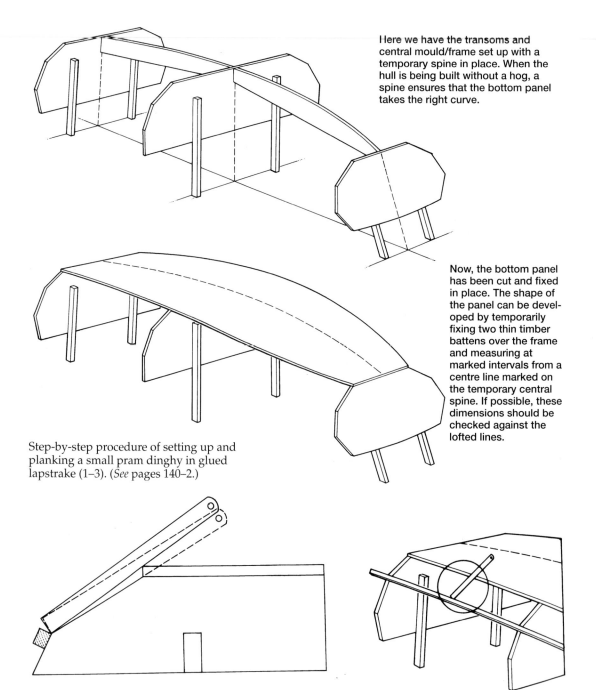

Here we have the transoms and central mould/frame set up with a temporary spine in place. When the hull is being built without a hog, a spine ensures that the bottom panel takes the right curve.

Now, the bottom panel has been cut and fixed in place. The shape of the panel can be developed by temporarily fixing two thin timber battens over the frame and measuring at marked intervals from a centre line marked on the temporary central spine. If possible, these dimensions should be checked against the lofted lines.

Step-by-step procedure of setting up and planking a small pram dinghy in glued lapstrake (1–3). (*See* pages 140–2.)

Once the bottom panel has been installed, the first pair of strakes can be shaped and glued in place. The first task, however, is to plane the bevels on the bottom panel by tacking a temporary batten to determine the top edges of the strakes – one either side. Then with one end of a straight edge against the inner edge of the batten, the other resting on the edge of the bottom panel, it is easy to see the angle that the bevel should be planed. Check frequently with the straight edge.

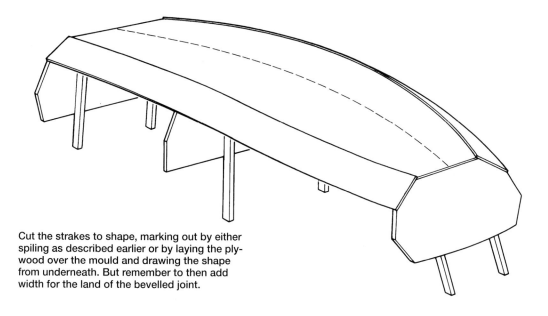

Cut the strakes to shape, marking out by either spiling as described earlier or by laying the plywood over the mould and drawing the shape from underneath. But remember to then add width for the land of the bevelled joint.

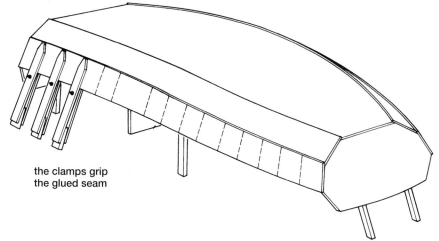

the clamps grip
the glued seam

The strake ends can be both glued and nailed in place but the lands that form the seams between the strakes are simply glued and, therefore, need clamping at close intervals. The clamps here are home-made from two pieces of timber, a nut and bolt and a wooden wedge.

Setting up and planking a small pram dinghy in glued lapstrake (4 & 5).

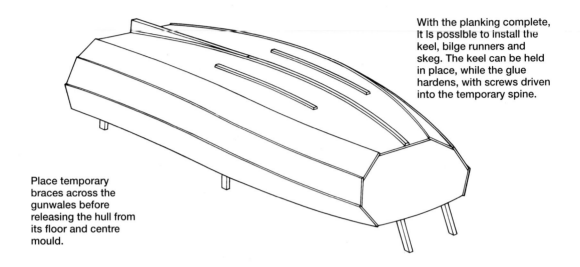

With the planking complete, It Is possible to install the keel, bilge runners and skeg. The keel can be held in place, while the glue hardens, with screws driven into the temporary spine.

Place temporary braces across the gunwales before releasing the hull from its floor and centre mould.

Setting up and planking a small pram dinghy in glued lapstrake (6).

plywood batten as a packing piece under the straight-edge. As a final guide to the alignment, two marks, a measured distance apart, can be made across the site of the scarf along the longitudinal line.

The sections of the strake can then be removed and aligned face-to-face using the edge tick marks to achieve a perfect alignment ready for the scarf to be cut and planed. When the joint is ready for gluing, the alignment can be checked by placing a straight-edge along the longitudinal line and measuring the space between the two gauging marks.

Marking Out the Garboard Strakes

Now we will take a more detailed look at marking and cutting the strakes. When working to a proprietary design, the width of the planks will probably be specified in some way: there may be fully dimensioned drawings of each strake, or simply

tick marks on each station frame to indicate the upper edge of each plank. Assuming the builder is faced by the latter, he or she must decide on the technique to adopt to transfer a shape bounded along one edge by the keelson and on the other by a line of pencil marks on the frames.

The first job is to ensure that the tick marks representing the upper edge of the garboard strakes (those furthest away from the keel) join up to make a fair curve. A simple way of doing that is to tack a flexible batten over the frames to join the marks, then to stand back and view the result: the batten should adopt a pleasing curve without any kinks. If not, identify the source of the problem and adjust the frame accordingly – and whatever is done on one side of the hull must be matched on the other.

We have now outlined the shape of the garboard strakes. The next task is to transfer that shape onto the plywood sheet that is to make up the first strake. There are a number of ways to do this, two of the most common being the direct or scribing method and he spiling method.

The Scribing Method

As the name suggests, the scribing method involves laying the plywood plank in position over the framework, and drawing or scribing the shape of the strake from below. The temporary batten tacked in place to define the upper edge of the garboard strake serves as a guide, whilst the keelson, stem and transom or stern post show the position of the other edges. However, it is not just that simple, because the plank would be stood off from the frames along its upper edge, yet snug down onto the keelson. The answer is to tack packing blocks along the keelson so that the plank is made to stand off the framework by a constant amount. It is then possible to mark an almost complete line along the upper edge of the strake, whilst the edge landing on the keelson will have a broken line, being drawn in at each packing block. Adjustment will also need to be made to allow for the width of the land to bear on the keelson. When this is done, a continuous line can be drawn in, using a flexible batten to join the points in a smooth curve.

The Spiling Method

The alternative spiling method is a little more involved and demands more in the way of spare timber, but it has the advantage of being approached completely from the outside of the framework – there is no need to crawl about to draw lines from underneath. As you will, by now, be fully aware that the strakes of a lapstrake hull are far from straight, so the spiling method may not prove as straightforward as the following description may suggest; with a

little ingenuity, however, it should go smoothly.

First, the edges of the proposed strake are marked along the keelson, frames, stem and stern; then a thin, wide batten is tacked over the frames inside the perimeter of the marks. Short cross-battens are clamped, and then tacked at intervals along the spiling batten, with the outer ends touching the marked lines on the framework – the tacking should be done when the spiling batten has been removed from the framework. The spiling batten is then placed over the strake blank and the shape of the plank transferred, making absolutely sure that the points are dropped down squarely and not at an angle. The points are then joined by connecting them with a flexible batten and lining in with a sharp pencil.

The strake can then be cut out, preferably using an electric jigsaw. If it has not already been scarf-jointed, this is the time to do it, using the techniques discussed earlier. The edges should be cleaned up using a finely set block plane.

Fitting the Garboard Strakes

The strake can now be offered up, aligning it with the guide marks drawn to coincide with the frames. It is very important that the strake should rest firmly against all the frames, and not be distorted amidships by forcing its ends into position without due regard to what the rest of it is doing. It is far better at this stage to adjust the position of the plank ends (hood ends) and have to trim a little off, than have the strake distorting under the pressure of attempting to close gaps between the strake and the amidships frames.

Once happy with the fit, the second garboard strake can be marked out and sawn.

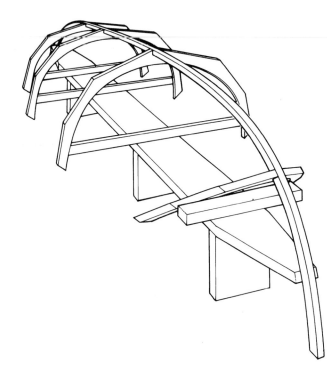

Laminated frames are first set up, along with hog and stems, on a heavy plank strongback.

Building a more traditional stem dinghy or, as here, a double-ender in lapstrake demands a different approach from that of pram dinghy building.

Rebates are cut into the top outer edge and the lower inner edge on all strakes except the top (sheer) strake and the very bottom (garboard) strake. They are rebated along the bottom inner and top outer edges respectively. The basic rebate should be planed, using a rebate plane, with the strake supported flat on a workbench. Where a bevel also has to be worked into the rebate, it is planed with the strake in position on the hull.

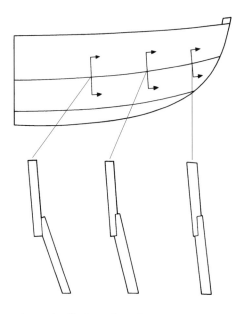

Fairing the lands as the strakes approach the stem: a rebate is gradually introduced into the bevel.

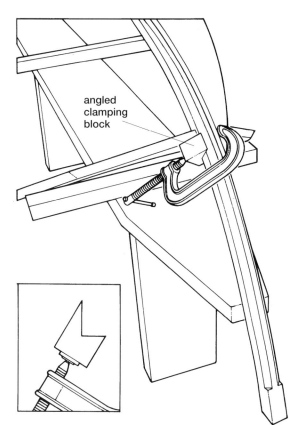

Clamping the strakes against the stem can be difficult because there is no parallel faces to screw the G-cramp against. The answer is to make a collection of angled, 'V'ed clamping blocks to go underneath the bottom of the cramp.

Being inventive when clamping strakes.

But instead of lifting the shape from the framework once more, the first strake can be used as a pattern. When making up the second of a pair, however, it is vital to work on a flat surface which supports the strakes over their entire length. Before finally fitting the garboards in place, their upper edges (furthest away from the keelson) must be rebated at the ends to take the following strakes. This is done using a rebate plane, with the fence set to the width of the land.

The garboards are now ready to be glued and screwed in place. If an epoxy glue is being used, it is important not to over-estimate the quantity needed. Once the epoxy is thoroughly mixed, speed is vital – when it is in the mixing pot the epoxy can generate a great deal of heat that speeds up curing, but once spread out over the framework, the reduction in volume reduces the speed of reaction, giving valuable extra time before it begins to set.

Making the Subsequent Pair of Strakes

These are marked out and made in exactly the same way as the garboards, except that each end of the strake needs to be rebated both top and bottom. It is much safer, at this point, to mark the rebates before cutting, and double check that they are being cut on the right side of the strake. Getting that part wrong can prove expensive in time and materials.

Before the second strakes are finally glued and fastened in place, the existing rebates in the garboards must be bevelled to accept the second strakes, and the full-length bevels must be planed between the rebates to accommodate the angle of the subsequent strake. This done, work can continue until the sheer strakes are reached. It is then important to remember that these strakes only require rebating on their lower inside edge!

Fitting Out

With the planking complete, the hull can be released from its temporary frames, turned the right way up, and then fitted out with thwarts, knees and centreboard box, following the same procedure as already described.

145

8 Strip Planking

Not so long ago, strip planking was regarded as a technique only suitable for larger hulls. However, developments in the use of epoxy and glass in conjunction with strip planking and more sophisticated cedar strip sections have enabled the building of much lighter boats. Now, it is not uncommon to encounter Canadian canoes built in cedar strip with planking less than ⅜in (10mm) thick. But to understand the process fully, it is worth going back to the beginnings of strip planking, to consider not only its benefits but also its shortcomings. And although it is possible for the amateur boatbuilder/designer either to build or design, or to adapt a design to strip planking, it is far more likely that he or she will follow a stock design.

TRADITIONAL STRIP PLANKING

Strip planking has been around for a long time; indeed the American writer, Howard I. Chapelle, expounds enthusiastically about the technique for amateur builders in his book, *Boatbuilding*, first published in 1941. But that was before the evolution of water-resistant adhesives, which opened up a whole range of new possibilities. The type of planking Chapelle talked about was a direct development of conventional carvel construction. By making the planks narrower, it became possible to bend them in both directions, allowing the use of parallel planking and so avoiding the need to

cut them to shape. It would, of course, be totally impractical to caulk such a hull to keep it watertight, so instead the seams were luted with a mix of thick paint that effectively sealed them for life. The luting didn't hold the planks together, however; that was the sole purpose of edge-nailing each plank to its neighbour, the nails sometimes passing through three or four planks; depending on the species of timber being used; soft-wood planking, for instance, needed longer nails.

The most common way of fitting one plank against the other was simply to bevel the mating edge of the adjoining plank. But even in those early days, some builders used the technique of rounding and hollowing the mating edges, because this was somewhat quicker than measuring and planing a bevel that changed its angle along the length of the hull. However, although it was quicker, the rounding-and-hollowing method did not totally overcome the problem of closing gap, especially on beamy hulls; and so finally, the bevelling method was considered a better proposition, producing a finer hull that needed less fairing off to produce a smooth finish.

The other problem to be overcome was that of the changing girth of the hull, which increases towards its centre sections. On a conventional carvel-packed hull, this is accommodated by shaping the individual planks, making them narrower at the ends. This often resulted in somewhat complicated shapes that were rather

Typical nail pattern on traditional strip planking. On modern strip planking the edge nails are replaced by a waterproof glue or epoxy.

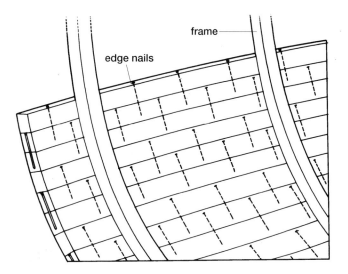

wasteful in terms of timber used – one of disadvantages of carvel construction that strip planking is supposed to obviate. The early approach was to use parallel-width planking down to the waterline, and then taper the planks to avoid introducing the need for excessive sideways bending. They also used a shaped gearboard strake (the plank that fits next to the keel) to take up some of the amidships girth.

There is, of course, no reason at all why conventional strip planking should not be used today. It does, however, have certain disadvantages, and its greatest as far as building is concerned, is its thickness: try and make it relatively thin and you immediately run into the problem of splitting the planks when nailing. Also, the nails must be sufficiently deep below the outside face of he hull so that it can be faired up, a process which can involve quite a lot of planing: if the nails were too near the surface you would risk taking chunks out of your best plane iron, besides which exposed nails are both unsightly and a possible source of weakness. Moreover

you certainly can't get them out easily, if at all.

This leads to the next big problem, which is the difficulty of cutting out and repairing conventional strip planking. Also potentially damaging are the stresses set up in a hull which is held rigidly together: unlike carvel or clinker planking where the hull is able to move and flex without losing watertight integrity, any movement in the timber of a strip-planked hull – due to a change in moisture content – is trapped, and this sets up stresses which, beyond a certain level, can cause cracking along the seams.

MODERN STRIP PLANKING

There is a great deal more to modern strip planking than just sticking the strips together with a waterproof glue: it encapsulates a whole new philosophy towards building a hull from wood, from the timber used for the planking to the way lightness is combined with strength, plus

147

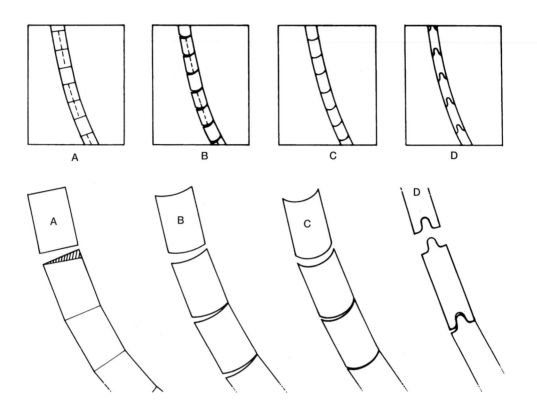

As each strip is fitted, its mating face would be planed to close the gap which would have been luted and the strip edge nailed.

By planing a straight-forward radius on the mating faces, the gap was minimized and a combination of gluing and edge nailing united the planks, one to the other.

A further development of the concave/convex mating faces created a section which could both take a curve and also form a closed joint. This is commercially known as 'Cedar Strip'.

A further development created 'Speed Strip', which not only forms a closed seam on a curve but is largely self aligning.

Different methods of making the joint between timber strips.

timber stability. Indeed it has been described as a form of composite, or sandwich construction, in which the timber constitutes only the core. Both lightness and stability come from an important development in the concept of strip planking, and that is the use of cedar instead of more traditional boat-building timbers such as mahogany. It is easy to understand how this has brought about a lighter craft;

the question of timber stability, however, is a little more subtle

Unlike any other timbers, when dried to between 8 to 10 per cent moisture content, western red cedar doesn't readily absorb moisture and so is less prone to swelling. and whilst clinker and carvel hulls rely on their planks swelling to tighten the hull and keep the water out, it is this very characteristic that can cause traditional strip planking to virtually self-destruct. The problem of weakness across the grain is solved by cross-grain reinforcement, which is where the composite structure concept comes from. There are two main options: either the cedar strip planking is sheathed with a layer of glass and epoxy resin, or it is reinforced by a layer of timber veneers, bonded to the hull at an angle of 45° to the direction of the strip planking. On larger hulls, combinations of the two are often used, creating a true sandwich with glass and epoxy on the outside. But on smaller hulls it is common practice to omit the layers of veneer and simply reinforce the strip planking with glass mat and epoxy.

Profiled Cedar Strip

The development that really made strip planking a viable method of construction for professional boatbuilders, and one that has made the job considerably easier for the amateur builder, has been the introduction of strip profiles that produce planking with closed seams – even when bent into a compound curve. There are various timber suppliers offering profiled sections; one of the first was offered by Joseph Thompson of Sunderland, a sophisticated concave/convex section which looks like a simple radius and is sometimes referred to as 'thumb-nail profile'. Its main drawback is that it has feather edges on the concave faces, which can be easily damaged; moreover, the strips must be scarfed together, should they need joining to give greater lengths, and this also slows down the planking process.

With these problems in mind, a more sophisticated section was developed: this looks like narrow tongue-and-groove boarding, but can be bent into compound curves, and is less vulnerable than its predecessor (which is still available). It is also

interlocking and produces a smoother surface needing far less fairing, and it can be butt jointed. All these qualities speed up the building time considerably and make the task easier.

SETTING UP

Although modern strip planking has moved on considerably, the actual techniques of planking have changed little – they have just got easier. We will therefore concentrate on modern cedar planking, with the occasional reference to the older style where relevant. Another point to consider at this time is which way up to build the hull: if we were to follow carvel building tradition, it would be the right way up – gunwales uppermost. Certainly this avoids the problem of having to turn the boat over when planking is completed, and it also gives far better access to inside the hull for cleaning up the glue joints as work progresses – however, it makes it all but impossible to apply the outer layer of glass mat and epoxy, and also more difficult to make sure that the seams in the bottom sections of the hull are completely closed. So for practical purposes, the hull should be built upside-down.

There are two basic approaches to strip planking a small boat: the first is to build the hull over a temporary mould made from cheap timber and chipboard; when it is complete, fit it out by adding the internal furniture, having discarded the building frame or stored it away in preparation for building another hull. The other approach, sometimes referred to as the 'egg-box' method, is to build the internal framework – the bulkheads, seat sides and so on – and with that fixed firmly as a base, lay up the planking directly over the bulkheads.

The disadvantage of the first approach is that there is really no such thing as cheap timber, and it does seem unethical to throw away perfectly good wood. Also, to achieve a fair hull, the moulds must be relatively closely spaced, far closer than is necessary for the structural integrity of the boat. On the other hand, some argue that the 'egg-box' method produces a boat that has a more complicated internal structure than it needs. And because the permanent framework has to be built from quality materials, the extra cost involved with this 'egg-box' method is likely to be greater than the cost of a temporary building frame. But here again, if you are working to a bought design, the decision will probably have been made by the designer.

If building over a temporary frame, the early stages of construction follow the same basic steps as for building almost any hull made over a frame: frame moulds are first cut out from lofted lines, or full-size patterns (if you are working to a modern design), taking the form of a series of equally spaced moulds over which the strip planking is laid. As we have said, closely spaced moulds give the best chance of producing a fair hull. As a guide, a hull less than say, 18ft (5.5m) overall, should have building frames spaced at about 18in (45cm) intervals, whilst larger craft can be built satisfactorily with building frames spaced progressively more widely.

DIFFERING GIRTH

The girth of the hull is far greater amidships than towards the ends. On traditional strip-planked hulls, there was little problem in tapering the planks or even adding in a stealer (a short section of tapered planking to make up extra width) to accommodate the differences in girth between the stem and the stern; but with specially profiled planking strips, it is not at all practical to taper planks. So we need to work in such a way as to minimize the effects of planking with parallel strips. It has been suggested that 95 per cent of modern hulls can be strip planked using parallel strips without having to make any special provisions; it just takes some careful planning and a little forethought. So let us first consider the consequences of the various options.

Start planking at the keel, and by the time you reach the gunwale, the planking will have adopted a very unsightly curve. On the other hand, begin at the gunwale and the unsightly curve doesn't begin to develop to any degree until work has progressed beneath the waterline.

One could quite rightly ask why it matters, provided the strips can be persuaded to adopt the necessary curves involved, especially if the outside of the hull is to be painted. If a great deal of care is taken over sanding and fairing off the outside of the planking, the glued seams may well be invisible – for a while at least. But in time, it is likely that the seams will show through, and if they are not sympathetic to the run of the topsides, they can spoil the appearance of the boat.

The way to get a good idea as to how the planking will appear is by stepping off the positions of the seams on the edges of the building-frame moulds. Start at the gunwale and work towards the keel: you will reach the keel first where the stem forefoot meets the keel, then the transom, followed by the point of greatest beam. To start with, it is perhaps best to face the edges of the moulds with masking or drafting tape so that if at first you don't like the results, subsequent attempts can be made without

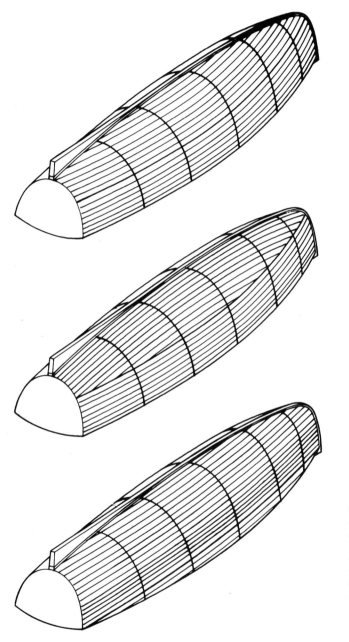

Starting the planking parallel with the gunwale results in a pronounced curve in the strip planking at the keel.

One solution is to plank up the hull in two sections working towards a bilge stringer.

On small boats, however, it is possible to attack the first strip at a slight curve to the gunwale. This means that the strips will take a 'straighter' line around the bilge.

The reason for taking care over the way the strips lie on the hull is largely for aesthetics, even if the hull is painted, the seams can show – even through a coat of glass cloth and resin. Planking that generally follows parallel with the waterline looks best.

Even on a slim pilling dinghy there is a significant difference between the girth amidships and at the ends of the hull.

151

confusion, simply by replacing the tape each time.

It is possible to place a batten over the moulds in order to discover the natural lie of a plank just above the waterline; mark its position, and you can use that as a datum and work outwards towards the gunwale and the keel, producing an aesthetically pleasing result and minimizing the degree of sideways bend at the keel. If the design doesn't specify the starting point, then it is worth taking a little trouble to explore the possibilities.

There are some hull shapes, however, that simply defy the straightforward approach. Excessively beamy hulls or those with traditional wine-glass sections can prove particularly vexing, in which case a more subtle approach is called for. A bilge stringer can offer a solution: the stringer extends the full length of the hull and has to be let into the moulds, or bulkheads, when using the egg-box method. Planking starts at the gunwale and works towards the stringer, finishing along its centre line. The second section of planking is then started from the keel, working downwards towards the stringer. In some circumstances it may even be desirable to include two longitudinal bilge stringers to accommodate a difficult shape. But wherever possible take the easy option, which is to start from the gunwale and work towards the keel.

PLANKING DETAILS

Having decided upon the planking regime, the time has come to make a start – but not before assembling the kit of tools needed for the task. Ideally you should have two cordless electric drills, one for drilling holes, the other for driving screws.

You will also need containers for measuring and mixing the epoxy resin. The third and extremely important requirement is protection against the epoxy for both the planking team and the tools. For the people involved, the minimum is overalls and protective gloves, but check the resin-maker's recommendations as to the safe use of the product. Where possible, the tools should be covered in plastic bags, although be careful to leave clear any air vents on electric tools; when you get into the swing, these will be working hard and blocked air vents will cause overheating!

Making a Start

Let's assume that we are using one of the modern profiled strips – where possible use full-length strips. But if, to save waste, some joints are included, make sure they are well spread out for both aesthetic and structural reasons – especially when using the type of section which needs only butt joints.

Make one last check that the edges of any temporary frames are well covered in plastic adhesive tape to prevent them becoming a permanent part of the hull structure, then offer up the first strip. Although it is possible to work alone at this stage, it is far better to have a team of at least two pairs of hands, especially when approaching the keel where an appreciable amount of sideways bend has to be applied to the strip. Place the strip with the groove uppermost: this will encourage glue to run into, rather than out of the seam, and so will obviate glue starvation.

This first strip will be glued, and either screwed or ring-nailed to the stem and transom. Some suggest that screwing is better because it gives better control in an area where splitting is a real risk. Either way, it is important to drill a pilot hole for the fastening. If the strip is to run perfectly parallel with the gunwale, remember to leave a little along the top edge for trimming off square. Where the strip rests against the frame moulds, it must be secured to take the pressure off the next strip; simply screw it to the mould, preferably using a multi-start wood screw with a washer behind its head to spread the pressure. The disadvantage of this procedure is that it leaves a line of holes which must subsequently be filled. Normally, however, this will not create a problem because they will be covered by the cross-grain reinforcement, which is then painted.

The Smaller Boat

When building a small boat using light sections, it is possible to fix the strips temporarily in place with staples fired in over a fabric tape to assist withdrawal. It is also possible to clamp the strips in position, but it would be far more time-consuming, and it would mean that you would have to wait until the glue had set before you could continue. If the hull is being planked in 'thumb-nail' section strips it is possible to edge-nail as in the older forms of strip planking; although some would argue – with some justification – that the greatest virtue of modern strip planking is that it is not edge-nailed and can therefore be repaired more easily.

Symmetrical Work

In most forms of boat building it is a good idea to work symmetrically so that the stresses on both sides of the hull develop evenly. Cedar strip planking is no exception. Working on both sides in turn also enables you to see that the job is progressing evenly, and if it is not, to find out why.

So, once the first strip has been located on one side of the building frame, repeat the process on the other side. You will then be ready to add further strips, working evenly towards the keel, installing perhaps two or three strips on one side, then moving to the other to even up progress. Once the glue has set, there is no real reason why the majority of the fixing screws should not be removed for re-use on subsequent sections.

Mixing Epoxy

At this stage you must learn to develop the technique of measuring, mixing and spreading just sufficient of the epoxy resin to do the job in hand. When mixing epoxy, it is vital to get the quantities of the two-part mix exactly right. Different brands of epoxy call for different ratios of resin and hardener, and unlike polyester resin – the 'other' resin used in making glass-reinforced plastics (GRP) and tolerant to variations in the proportions of resin to hardener – there is nothing to be gained by adding a little more in order to speed up, or reducing it to slow things down: the consequence will only be a reduction in the strength of the joint. And as it is only the epoxy holding a lot of modern boat hulls together it is vital to mix the resin and hardener properly and in the right proportions. But thanks to various pieces of measuring equipment offered by resin suppliers this is not difficult. Follow the makers' instructions and all will be well.

The same applies to the addition of filler materials to the epoxy to modify its character, making it suitable for use as wood adhesive. By itself, epoxy resin would drain away from the seam and would not have sufficient body to cure properly. The addition of various powder fillers provides body and gives the resin the necessary consistency for it to cure fully and develop its maximum strength potential.

As we have said, of equal importance is not to mix too much epoxy for the job in hand; experience will show how much is needed for a particular job. Mix a third too much, and the cost of the resin to build the hull increases by a third – and where epoxy is concerned, that can be a significant sum, even on a relatively small hull.

Final Stages

As work progresses, the sideways curve on each strip will increase, which will make it all the more important to ensure that sufficient pressure is being applied to close the gaps. The danger here is that in pulling the strip into position, the profiled edge may be damaged. This can be avoided by having a few short lengths of strip to slot over the one being bent; you can even cut the rear edges of the pads to form wedges which can be inserted between the planking strip and temporary stops clamped to the moulds.

It is far easier to trim the strip ends at the stem and transom as the planking progresses. When the keelson is reached, the ends of the strips must be angled to set fair against the line of the keel. This can involve some careful work, and it is usually necessary to close the final gap with a specially shaped strip. Although the strip itself can be offered up for marking with a pencil from beneath, it may be easier to make a template from hardboard or similar, that can be cut to shape easily. In theory, both final strips should be the same on both sides of the hull; in practice, however, this is very unlikely, so don't make the mistake of cutting two from a template which you have only fitted on one side. Marking the positions of the strips on the moulds should minimize the difference.

FAIRING AND FINISHING

If the work has been done carefully and the surplus glue removed before it hardened, the hull should not need too much fairing up. Inevitably, however, there will be some glue which needs removing, and the best tool for this task is a cabinet maker's scraper. Once down to wood, all that may be needed is a very thorough sanding with the glass paper held on a long, flexible sanding batten. In cases of extreme need, a finely set plane can be used; however, take care that you don't get carried away, because you may end up removing far more timber than was originally intended.

Electric sanders can be used to good effect, but avoid the simple disc sander – not only does it leave distinctively ugly circular sanding marks, it can also create a very uneven surface if not controlled carefully. Hand finishing may be the more laborious, but it can definitely produce the most reliable results.

When the hull is fair to the eye and the fingertips, the next task is applying the cross-grain reinforcement.

The Cross-grain Reinforcement

Using Veneer

Specialist timber suppliers offer veneers cut specifically for this job, usually in mahogany. It is applied to the strip-planked hull in strips of, typically 3 to 5in (7.6 to 12.7cm) wide, depending on the size and fullness of the hull. Obviously using wider strips reduces the amount of work involved. It is a compromise between speed, and persuading the strips to lie tightly over the compound curve of the hull without needing too much fairing.

The veneers are applied in two stages: the first are attached by gluing parallel-sided strips at approximately 45° to the direction of the strip planking and spaced so that the second application can be fitted snugly between to complete the layer. The most convenient method of holding the veneer strips whilst the glue is setting is with temporary staples. The second application is fitted by offering up the strips over the gaps between the first set, and marking their widths using a simple width gauge. The strips are then glued in place. When the glue has cured, the surface must be faired by hand-sanding.

Using Glass and Epoxy

The use of glass and epoxy for cross-grain reinforcement is a far more practical solution. When buying the materials, however, it is worth mentioning to the supplier their intended purpose, because there are glass mats which are right for the job, and others that are not. For instance, chopped strand mat, intended for making GRP, is held together by a powder specifically intended to be compatible with polyester resin: this mat is simply not suitable for use with epoxy resins.

The problem for the amateur, however, is that although the learning curve is a steep one, there are a few pitfalls that could turn the job into a disaster. Its whole success depends on pre-planning, having everything in its place and everything ready. Start by draping the glasscloth over the hull to establish the most convenient panel size. Small hulls may well be sheathed straight off in two halves; although the larger the panel of cloth, the more difficult it is to control.

The cloth can be applied with the hull either wet with resin, or with it dry; each

method has its virtues and potential problems, and until you try both, it is very difficult to say which is easier. The design may also call for the hull to be pre-coated with epoxy which is allowed to harden, but not left to cure completely before the glass cloth is applied.

The wet method of applying the glass cloth involves coating the hull with epoxy and laying the cloth onto the wet surface, rolling and stippling it to bring the epoxy through to the surface. If the job is done satisfactorily, the white appearance of the glass mat will disappear, giving way to almost complete transparency. White patches or even small flecks indicate that the cloth has not been completely saturated; these are weak points that will require more attention in order to eradicate entrapped air and consolidate the lamination. You need to add more resin at this point, because it may be resin starvation which is responsible for the lack of saturation. However, adding too much resin can float the glass away from the surface of the hull, producing a 'resin-rich' layer which lacks an intimate bonding between timber and glass mat. The rule is to use as little resin as possible commensurate with a complete lack of white patches, however small.

The advantage of laying the glass onto wet resin is that it guarantees to keep the resin between the glass and the hull. The disadvantage is that if you don't place the glass cloth in precisely the right place first time, repositioning it can be all but impossible. In any event, should you need to remove the wet cloth from the hull, it is an incredibly messy operation. Having a reliable helper close to hand can save the day.

The dry method of applying the cloth makes it easier to handle the materials, but the possible problem here is dry patches where the resin has not permeated fully through to the timber. The procedure is similar to applying the cloth over wet resin. Some advocate giving the hull a pre-coating of epoxy which is allowed to part-cure before laying the cloth in place. If the resin is worked thoroughly through the cloth, however, the only difference is a slightly higher resin-to-glass ratio.

As always, preparation is the key, and it is certainly an advantage to have help at hand to mix the resin and hold things. Once the glass-cloth panels have been cut to size, they are draped over the hull, if necessary, using the masking tape to hold them in position. The epoxy is then mixed and applied over the cloth. There are various ways of doing this, but a convenient method is to pour small puddles of resin onto the cloth and work it into the surface using a plastic spatula or soft-edged squeegee. Where two panels of glass cloth come together, a simple butt joint is sufficient on a small boat. On larger hulls, however, the designer may specify an overlap.

FINISHING AND REMEDIAL WORK

If, when the resin has cured, small areas are discovered where the glass has not bonded fully to the wood, resin can be injected through a small cut made in the surface. Larger areas should be removed and reglassed.

Additional coats of resin can be applied and the surface sanded to produce a smooth surface. When sanding, use fine grit paper and be very careful not to cut into the glass cloth. Careful finishing can produce a result that shows the full character of the timber, leaving the glass and resin exterior virtually invisible. The hull can now be removed from the building frame and the inside cleaned of any glue runs; it can then be lightly sanded, followed by an epoxy coating.

Thus encapsulated, the cedar planking will remain stable, and the stresses encountered with traditional forms of strip planking will not be set up. Fitting out can now proceed, installing all the usual components such as gunwales, thwarts, knees, breast hooks and so on.

9 Finishing Off

Paint technology has come a long way in the last decade or so, and it is certainly not the case nowadays that those who own a wooden boat spend all their time with paint brushes in their hands. However, it is possible, nonetheless, to let yourself be somewhat carried away by the technology of modern paint systems, and to forget why we spend so much time and money spreading what must sometimes seem like liquid gold on our boats. The purpose of painting and varnishing a boat is to protect it against the elements and to enhance its beauty, and whilst there is no reason not to have both as objectives, it is the first that should take precedence.

There is a strong feeling amongst some wooden boat enthusiasts that wood should always be seen in its natural state, thus advocating varnish only as a finish. This has perhaps evolved through a determination that a wooden boat should not look like a plastic one. If a boat is covered in paint, how do you know that it is actually built of wood? There are two answers: first, the really important differences are not disguised by a good coat of paint; and second, often painting a wooden boat is to be recommended because, on the whole, it provides better protection. That is not to say that modern marine varnishes don't do an excellent job: I am simply suggesting that we should think of the practicalities and not be swept away on a tide of false nostalgia.

THE IMPORTANCE OF PREPARATION

To achieve a really good finish, there is no doubt that thorough preparation is the key. This means removing all the lumps and bumps created by glue squeezed from joints, and giving the surface a good sanding and clean down before even thinking about applying paint or varnish. At this point it is also worth considering applying a rot inhibitor (wood preserver) to any timber that you may feel is vulnerable – although before you start, check that it is compatible with the sealant or paint you intend to use by trying out a test panel. The main thing is to follow the paint manufacturer's recommendations.

WHAT TYPE OF PAINT?

Look along the shelves of any yacht chandler and this will give you some idea of the choice available. Most paint manufacturers offer advice leaflets that are worth considering, but at the end of the day, you must make a reasoned choice, bearing in mind that the most expensive is not always the best, and that the cheapest is not always so in the long run.

Many owners claim that they have used a brand of household paint with total success and at far less cost, and are very happy with the results. However, if you were to inspect two boats, side by side, one painted with household paint, the other in top quality marine paint, the difference would show, and especially at the end of the season. But does this matter? Quite often the answer is 'No'. On a simple plywood dinghy that was built to be used rather than admired, the saving in cost is usually more important that achieving the best 'yacht' finish. If, on the other hand, you have built your boat with an epoxy coating, then the paint system you choose must be compatible with the epoxy, which usually means opting for one of the modern polyurethane paint systems.

The same applies to varnishes. The expensive products will probably last longer and involve less frequent repainting, whilst the less sophisticated paints may work out cheaper in the short term, but will probably involve more work eventually, and will not provide such lasting good looks. But on a small boat, is this important?

The most important factor is to look after the boat sensibly. So avoid parking it unprotected beneath an apple tree in the autumn, because you can hardly then expect to find it in good condition in the spring. Instead, repair the season's damage to the paint and varnish, and tuck her away safely so she is protected from the elements. The following spring, you will be ready to take to the water once more with the minimum amount of preparation and repainting.

Index